FAIREY IIIF
INTERWAR MILITARY WORKHORSE

Philip Jarrett

PUBLICATIONS

Contents

AUTHOR'S COLLECTION

Introduction

FEW British interwar military aircraft can claim to have given such wide and valuable service as the Fairey IIIF. This curiously unnamed aerial workhorse served in large numbers with both the Royal Navy and Royal Air Force from the late 1920s until the late 1930s—only a decade, perhaps, but ten years that saw the transition from wooden airframes to metal, and ten years that witnessed great military aviation activity across the British Empire.

From Great Britain to the Middle East and Far East, the Fairey IIIF was to be found flying from both land and water, serving at RAF bases, both in landplane and seaplane form, and also at naval bases and on board aircraft carriers, capital ships and cruisers, again in both forms. Its versatility enabled it to perform a variety of rôles—general-purpose aircraft, ambulance, bomber, carrier-borne or catapult-launched reconnaissance seaplane, gunnery spotter and target tug or glider-target launcher.

This spread: Three Gosport-based IIIFs—Mk IIIBs S1523 and S1784 and Mk I S1169—photographed in 1931 or 1933.

Evolved from a World War I design, the IIIF incorporated Richard Fairey's concept of streamlining, brought about by the lessons learned at the 1923 Schneider Trophy contest at Cowes, where he encountered the elegant Curtiss CR-3 racing seaplane with its compact and close-cowled, water-cooled Curtiss D-12 inline engine. Thus inspired, Fairey produced the Fox day bomber, an aircraft that easily outpaced pursuing fighters.

When, in the mid-1920s, Fairey came to develop his Rolls-Royce Eagle/Napier Lion-engined IIID dating from the end of World War I, he incorporated the lessons learned in producing the Fox. Although the 'broad arrow' form of the Napier Lion engine caused greater head resistance than 'vee'-form inlines, Fairey succeeded in cleaning up the IIID by careful streamlining, fairing and attention to detail. The resulting IIIF, while initially retaining some of the familiar lines of its forebear (especially in its tail surfaces), was distinctly more elegant, and also much more practical in terms of accessibility and maintainability.

A few final touches, brought in of necessity, resulted in an even better-looking aircraft. The IIIF was liked by pilots, and benefited from a high-lift wing incorporating Fairey's patent camber-changing flaps and, if included, the company's special mounting for the rear-cockpit gun, which was far less 'draggy' than the established Scarff ring. Unusually, the IIIF served with both the Royal Navy and the RAF at a time when, apart from a couple of designs from Hawker (which, incidentally, owed their origins to the concept behind the Fox), the two Services tended to operate different aircraft types. The other classic British military general-purpose aircraft of the period, the Westland Wapiti, never saw Royal Navy service.

Curiously, while the fitting of Handley Page slots (or 'slats'—both terms were in contemporary use) was decidedly beneficial to most aircraft types, their belated addition to the IIIF's upper wing outer leading edge seems to have had a detrimental, perhaps even dangerous, effect on the aircraft's behaviour at low speed and in the stall and spin.

In a time when foreign orders were not in great abundance, the IIIF nevertheless found military buyers in several countries, serving in Argentina, Chile, Greece and

5,000 feet), and its handling was acceptable despite longitudinal instability and heavy ailerons. Late that same year Mk IIIB S1474, strengthened for catapulting, was also the subject of handling tests, and an initial assessment of flotation gear was made using S1226. The latter tests resulted in the rejection of the installation, as the two bags stowed beneath the wings, which took fifty seconds to inflate, were too weak. Consequently a new fuselage stowage on the fuselage of S1504 was evaluated in 1931. Although it was an improvement, in the ditching trial the cock that released the compressed air to inflate the bags needed one and a half turns to operate in the final seconds before impact. Moreover, once the aircraft had settled in the water its pilot could not get to the dinghy. The aircraft was recovered, and ditched again on 7 May after modification, this time satisfactorily.

One of the small seven-aircraft batch of Mk IIIB (DC) dual-control trainers, S1847, underwent FAA evaluation and spinning tests at the A&AEE in July 1934, after being returned to Fairey and fitted with a blind-flying hood and equipment. Handling trials, spins and dives to 206mph with the hood both stowed and raised brought no adverse comments.

In a Spin

Testing for the Services

AT the end of 1927 N225 was fitted with floats at Hamble, and it was later given wings with Handley Page slats. It was modified to become the all-metal Mk IIIM, with a trial installation of the Lion XIA. On 5 March 1928 it, too, went to the MAEE for tests as a seaplane. The adoption of this engine, plus manufacturing changes, delayed the first production IIIM's maiden flight until 26 March 1929. In 1930 N225 returned to Felixstowe fitted with the 480hp Rolls-Royce F.XII (Kestrel II), one of three similar IIIFs (see below, pages 206–209). On this visit its three aerodynamic controls were deemed heavy, which made flying in bumpy air and in the glide difficult. Long flights were made tiring by the longitudinal instability and sluggish elevator.

Although tests with a model at the National Physical Laboratory had suggested that the IIIF seaplane would not be dangerous to spin, it was realised that the margin of safety would be less than for the landplane version. Consequently, Mk IIIM S1316, now fitted with floats, underwent spinning trials in the first half of 1931. The standard auto-slots fitted were inefficient, and the aircraft was very

Below and right: The second prototype N225 as an FAA three-seater with the interim angular fin and unbalanced rudder. These photographs were taken during trials at Martlesham Heath.

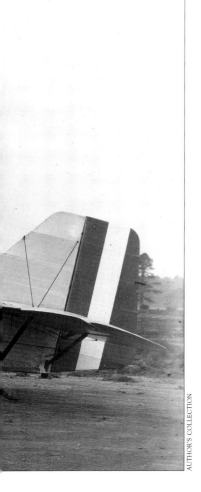

unstable in roll and barely controllable when gliding at incidences of 30 degrees or more, exhibiting a tendency to spin. The glides were then discontinued so that short spins could be made at a higher altitude than was reached at the end of the glides. With forward centre of gravity, easy and rapid recovery was made from spins of three or four turns to the left and right. However, when spin recovery was attempted after three or four turns with the CG aft, the aircraft would not recover, and the crew was obliged to bale out. (This event is described by Flight Lieutenant Pickering and Woodward Nutt on pages 66–67.) It was concluded that 'the IIIF seaplane might develop a dangerous spin after two or three turns, even with forward c.g.', and as a result the tests were discontinued.

However, as the IIIF was by this time a widely used Service aircraft, the test establishments did not abandon their investigations of its behaviour at the low end of the speed range. In February 1932 further full-scale tests of behaviour at high angles of incidence were initiated, the aircraft used being IIIF Mk IIIM seaplane S1340, with a Lion XIA. Model tests had indicated that, owing to the large positive pitching moments caused by the floats, incidences as high as 49 degrees were possible. At the outset the full-scale tests were mostly conducted by Flying Officer Frank

Whittle (later to pioneer the turbojet engine) and Flight Lieutenant Leslie S. Snaith (later to join the High Speed Flight).

With the engine switched off, the radiator fully retracted, the flaps set at zero and the tail trim set at neutral, measurements were made of the aircraft's inclination to the horizontal, the elevator angle, the rate of descent and the airspeed (recorded by a strut-mounted swivelling log). Fitted with standard IIIF wings, S1340 was tested in engine-off glides and at incidences of over 35 degrees, and in two glides at about 50 degrees, when the rate of descent was 4,690 feet per minute (53.3mph). The seaplane proved so violently unstable both laterally and longitudinally that it was barely controllable.

The tests continued until March 1933, and S1340 was then fitted with upper wings modified by the Royal Aircraft Establishment, having revised tops and more efficient auto-slots. When testing resumed in June and July the aircraft was still markedly unstable longitudinally, though the motion was less violent owing to lower rates of rotation in roll. However, it was somewhat more stable laterally. The highest achievable incidence was about 40 degrees. The improvement in behaviour with the RAE wings was attributed to less violent instability, improvement in technique and higher accuracy of observation. The results agreed more closely with the model test predictions, and confirmed the high pitching moment of the floats.

Below: Late in 1929 Fairey re-engined N225 with a Rolls-Royce F.XII/Kestrel engine, at the same time fitting the now-standard IIIF fin and rudder. Further pictures of this version appear on page 207–208.

Above and left: The steel-winged Fairey IIIF Mk IIIB S1835 on the MAEE slipway at Felixstowe in 1933, during trials with a single central main float and small stabilising wingtip floats.

Another essential trial was that carried out to assess the effectiveness of the flotation gear installed in the IIIF landplane. For this exercise, S1504, with full fuel tanks and a take-off weight of 6,003 pounds, was deliberately ditched in Harwich harbour on 26 January 1931, into a 15–20mph wind and with eighteen-inch-high waves. After impact the aircraft stood vertically for a moment and then floated for three hours with its upper wing awash and its fuselage submerged. The marine distress signals and the dinghy inflator were out of action, the tail lifting strop was not easily accessible, and the crew had to clamber on to the upper wing.

Above: Also seen at Felixstowe, S1532 displays an experimental float undercarriage reminiscent of that fitted to the earlier 'IIIs', with shorter main floats, an ungainly tail float and auxiliary wingtip floats.
Below: A further view of S1532 at Felixstowe, clearly showing its experimental floats.

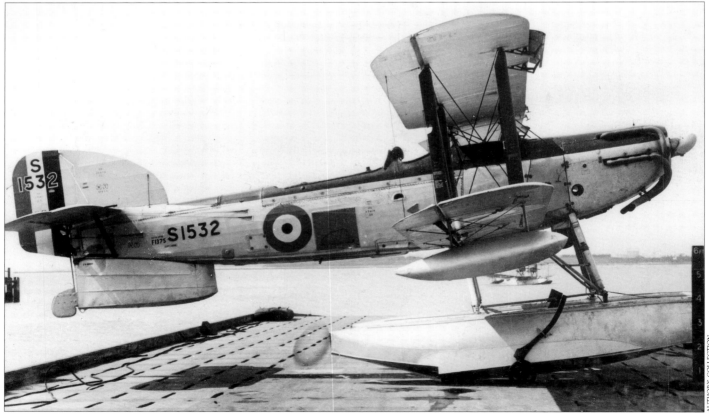

The greatest damage was probably inflicted by the heavy anchor-type chain used to lift S1504 out of the water.

The fin and rudder of prototype and early-production IIIFs followed the design of the familiar rectangular-outline unit used on all previous Fairey aircraft, though a horn-balanced rudder of higher aspect ratio was fitted. As recounted above, however, it transpired that the float-equipped IIIF would not fly straight at full power, even with full bungee trim and right rudder pressure held, and that, even at cruising speeds, a large amount of right rudder was required. Following tests of a variety of alternative shapes, including a plain high-aspect-ratio form fitted to N225, surfaces with a more aesthetic, elliptically curved outline were adopted, the rudder having an inset aerodynamic balance. The original form of the revised vertical surfaces, rather squarer than the configuration ultimately adopted, were initially tested on a landplane IIIF. When the rudder proved to be of insufficient area, the larger of the two versions offered was tested on the first prototype, N198, at the MAEE in the autumn of 1927, to determine whether directional control on the floatplane version was effective. Although bigger angles were needed with the new rudder to obtain the same control effect, adequate movement was available, there were no rudder loads at cruising speeds, and only a small amount of rudder was required at full power. Even so, while some earlier machines were retrofitted with the new vertical tail, others retained their original, angular units.

Further MAEE tests continued throughout 1928, float design proving particularly problematic. At the MAEE, N198 was fitted with new, high-buoyancy, metal floats on a rigid undercarriage structure. However, these floats suffered structural failure during two series of tests, and even after they had been strengthened they proved to give an extremely harsh ride in any disturbed water. Attempts to resolve this problem by fitting rubber-ball-type shock absorbers and, later, oleos, were unsuccessful, and even though further tests in 1928, entailing some fifty alightings, proved the floats' robustness, they were still harsh-riding. This was attributed to the design of their undersurface, but by now the MAEE's

Left, upper and lower: These photographs of Fairey IIIF Mk IIIM S1336 at the MAEE are date-stamped '6 Jan 1930'. The aircraft was at Felixstowe in December 1929, when its performance with a Lion XIA proved disappointing, its 'very heavy' controls making controllability poor and therefore unsatisfactory for the RAF. Ease of maintenance was praised, but there was evidence of rapid corrosion.

Left: S1336, seen here again at the MAEE in a print dated '6 Jan 1930', also underwent catapult trials with its 6,300-pound buoyancy floats. In 1931 the same aircraft was used to measure lift and drag in the glide with the propeller stopped and then at idling, the results agreeing with model tests.

test pilots had found that floats could be designed so that shock absorbers were unnecessary, and that, because shock absorbers gave the floats a freedom of angular movement that made accurate control difficult during take-off and alighting, a rigid attachment was better.

The MAEE tested different types of propeller on Mk IVC seaplane J9165, comparing a Fairey-Reed metal propeller of six inches greater diameter than standard, and a special Fairey-built, wooden propeller, with the standard IIIF Fairey-Reed propeller. The two new propellers were found to be so superior to the standard unit that the IIIF seaplane's usefulness was greatly increased. Although the lighter wooden propeller produced the best all-round performance, the metal one was preferred owing to its greater prospective serviceability. Especially note-worthy was the improved take-off performance of 15.5 seconds in a ten-knot

Below and right, upper: IIIF Mk IVM J9164 at Martlesham Heath during tests of modified slats attached to the upper wing leading edges.

Above: J1964 again, here fitted with a pair of 75-gallon auxiliary fuel tanks beneath its lower wings which, not surprisingly, caused even further degradation of its performance. Notice also the added exhaust piping, directing the gases away from the fuselage

Left: An anonymous IIIF with what, in 1929, were described as 'bomb' tanks attached beneath its lower wings, in the positions normally occupied by bombs. These non-jettisonable auxiliary fuel tanks enabled the IIIF's range at cruising speed to be increased from some 700 miles, on internal tankage alone, to about 1,450 miles.

AUTHOR'S COLLECTION

wind, compared with 30 seconds with the standard propeller. This meant that the period during which solid water was thrown up into the propeller was greatly reduced, enabling the aircraft to operate in rougher sea conditions. An RAE-designed wooden propeller built for the same tests burst while it was being run up for the first time.

Other IIIFs tested at the MAEE included J9150, a Jupiter-engined aircraft used to test floats; S1340, a Mk IIIM with a Lion XIA, used for flight tests at high incidences with auto-slots; and S1504, which was used to assess the serviceability of stainless-steel wings and was also employed for the ditching trials in Harwich Harbour in 1931. The wings were also fitted to S1340, and after 93 hours of flying over thirteen months their condition was found to be excellent compared with the standard type, exhibiting marked resistance to corrosion. The wings were

Below: Fairey IIIF Mk IIIM S1317 leaves the compressed-air accelerator (catapult) at Farnborough during experiments carried out in 1930 in connection with the Fairey Queen radio-controlled target aircraft (see pages 194–205).

AUTHOR'S COLLECTION

then fitted to Mk IIIB S1835, which had a single main float and stabilising floats at the wingtips, and a further 92 hours of flying were completed. As the result of an accident on 13 December 1934 the wings were immersed in sea water for two and a half hours before the aircraft was salvaged, but it was found that the surface rust was easily removed and that such pitting as occurred was not deep. After the same set of wings had accumulated a total of 186 flying hours their condition was reported to be good, and far better than standard units that had been subjected to similar treatment. After such suffering, it was hardly surprising that S1835 became instructional airframe 739M in 1935.

The Mk IIIB S1532 served as a test-bed for a variety of items. In 1930 it was used as a mock-up for flotation gear; it was used to test bomb carriers, pioneering the Universal Carrier in 1932, and was with No 35 Squadron RAF and at Gosport later that year on these duties. From August to October 1932 it was involved in propeller tests at RAE Farnborough and with No 22 Squadron and at the A&AEE. There had been a persistent problem with vibration on the IIIF, and S1532 spent six months on trials of various Fairey Reed metal propellers, all of which were unsuccessful in relieving the problem. It was finally resolved by the use of a slightly finer Watts wooden propeller. In November 1932 Fairey fitted S1532 with short twin main floats, a deep IIID-type 'solid' tail float and strut-mounted wingtip floats. In this form it underwent trials at the MAEE from April 1933.

Top, and above left: In 1930 Fairey IIIF Mk I S1148, from the pre-production batch, was used to assess the practicability of seaplanes taking off and landing on carrier decks. The trials took place on board HMS *Furious*, the aircraft's floats having been reinforced for the task. Both of these pictures were taken during landings: the deck hands watching the seaplane making its landing approach are in for a spectacular display of sparks as the floats slide along the steel flight deck! Owing to the lack of control after touch-down, a very high standard of flying was required.

After being struck off charge at Felixstowe on 14 October 1935 it ended its life as a catapult dummy.

The A&AEE flew an unmarked, metal-framed IIIF with a Lion XA; two types of automatic slat were tested on S1208 in 1928, lateral control being maintained down to the stall, and ineffective heel-operated brakes were also tested on this machine; J9164, with modified slats, was tested later that year, but the altered slots remained open at too high an airspeed and never closed fully. In 1929 J9164 represented the standard Service IIIF GP with Frise ailerons, slats and increased weight. Trials with the same machine continued in 1930, as efforts were made to improve speed, ceiling and comfort, but with little success. The addition of two 75-gallon tanks beneath the lower wings degraded performance even further.

The Royal Aircraft Establishment at Farnborough carried out spinning tests of the IIIF using Mk I S1147 in 1929 and Mk IIIM S1317 in 1932 (see below, page 60 *et seq.*). The latter aircraft was also used at Farnborough for catapult-launching experiments in 1930, being mounted on a cradle that supported it at four points, and with its tailskid resting in a guide rail. The three-joint telescopic catapult ram was driven by compressed air contained in cylinders beneath the structure, and the aircraft had its Handley Page slots open during launch. On 28 January 1931 K1165, a Mk IVM, went to the RAE, where it was used for engine development and vibration tests and later undertook target-towing trials and was fitted with an anti-spinning tail parachute. It was then used for wire barrage trials, finally being struck off charge on 9 October 1936.

Other tests assessed the practicability of launching and landing seaplanes on carrier decks. These took place on *Furious* in 1930, using IIIF S1148, fitted with reinforced floats (and still with the original square-cut fin and rudder). To provide

Below: Before it went on board HMS *Courageous*, Mk IIIM S1354—seen here shortly after completion—was tested with an experimental tail unit at the A&AEE from September 1929. In 1932 it was loaned to the RAE at Farnborough to have a new type of arrester gear hook fitted.

Left: An engineless Fairey IIIF with its flotation bags deployed and inflated is prepared for ditching trials on board the catapult trials ship HMS *Ark Royal*. The airframe appears to have been stripped of useful components, even the tyres having been removed from the wheels. With the impending delivery to the Royal Navy of the new fleet carrier of the same name, *Ark Royal* was renamed *Pegasus* in December 1934.

AUTHOR'S COLLECTION

some initial impetus at the start of its take-off run the aircraft was rocked and given a strong push by the flight-deck party. Landing, with no arrester gear, was rather tricky owing to the lack of directional control. It must have been quite a spectacle, as the floats created a shower of sparks as the aircraft slid along the steel flight deck, and the aircraft usually ended its run near the deck's forward edge.

Apart from different engines being installed in IIIFs for non-Service buyers, several test-bed installations were made by the manufacturer. The liquid-cooled,

AUTHOR'S COLLECTION

635hp Rolls-Royce Kestrel II was flown in J9173, J9174 and N225, the last being tested at the MAEE in this form. In addition, J9174 was used for experiments with silencing equipment. The 460hp Armstrong Siddeley Jaguar VIC radial was fitted in J9154 in 1929, and the 525hp Panther IIA in both that machine and S1325, leading to the general-purpose Gordon for the RAF (many of which aircraft were converted from IIIFs) and the Seal for the FAA. In June 1928 a 520hp Bristol Jupiter VIII radial was flown in J9150, which was tested in both landplane and seaplane forms, and the RAE tested the Junkers Jumo 205C diesel in K1726 from 1936 to 1939 (see pages 208–213)

The basic variants of Service IIIFs were as follows: IIIF Mk I—initial production version for the FAA with metal fuselage and wooden wings; Mk II—as Mk I but with increased load factors; Mk IIIM—all-metal version; Mk IIIMDC—dual-control trainer variant of the Mk IIIM; Mk IIIB—as IIIM but strengthened for catapulting and incorporating other modifications; Mk IIIBDC—dual-control Mk IIIB; Mk IVC—composite-construction RAF version; Mk IVCM—as IVC but with minor structural changes and increased use of metal; Mk IVM—all-metal but for ribs in fin and rudder; Mk IVM/A—entirely all-metal structure; Mk IVB—to Specification 3/31, incorporating all of the modifications in the FAA Mk IIIBs.

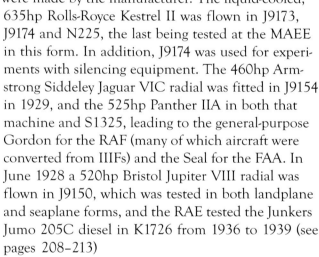

Anatomy of a Thoroughbred

The IIIF's Structure Described

THE fuselage of the Fairey IIIF Mk IV was built as a braced girder and was constructed in three portions. The front comprised the welded tubular steel engine mounting, each of the bearers being supported by a 'vee' formation of struts. The centre portion consisted of three bays, the second of which embodied the front and rear spar positions for the lower wings; the third bay formed the pilot's cockpit. Also included in this portion were the struts and framework for the centre section of the upper mainplane. The third fuselage unit (eight bays) was a wood- or wire-braced tubular structure containing the observer's cockpit and carrying the tail unit. Its top longerons overlapped Bay 3 of the centre portion. Bays 4 and 5 were occupied by the rear cockpit, the floor panel in Bay 4 being provided with a trapdoor for prone-position bomb aiming.

The engine and centre portions were covered by aluminium cowling panels held in place by spring-loaded locking clips. Aluminium covered the port side from the engine cowling to Frame 4, but on the starboard side it terminated at Frame 2, the remaining side panels of the centre portion being covered with laced fabric. The top-decking around the cockpits and the underside up to Frame 4 was also cowled with aluminium. The rear fuselage was contoured by light formers and stringers, and was fabric covered.

The land and float undercarriages were easily interchangeable. The former was of the through-axle type, with oleo legs as the front struts and radius rods with pivoted joints for the rear struts, which were cross-braced. The oleo leg contained two columns of rubber rings, air which could be compressed and oil which flowed through restricted orifices. The self-centring tailskid pivoted on a specially

Below: The cockpits of the three-seater variant of the IIIF, minus the pilot's seat. In the centre, folded up, is the observer's seat, and the gunner's seat, lowered, is to the rear.

Above: Here the retractable radiator can be seen low down between the rear of the engine and the firewall. The long metal channel along the fuselage side is the blast trough for the single fixed forward-firing Mk II Vickers 0.303 air-cooled machine-gun. The front,

faired oleo legs of the land undercarriage derived their shock-absorbing qualities from banks of rubber rings, air which could be compressed and the flow of oil through restricted orifices. The rear undercarriage struts were radius rods with pivoted joints.

Below: The central fuselage, with the upper wing centre section supported on cross-braced centre-section struts, the 45-gallon top main fuel tank and the 80-gallon bottom main tank. Immediately behind the head of the man in the bottom left-hand corner is the 9½-

gallon oil tank. The wheels at the front of the pilot's seat pan controlled the variable-incidence tailplane and the camber-changing flaps on the wing trailing edges; the wheel at the rear of the seat was the elevator cam.

drives and actuating screws operated the flaps through cables. The flaps could move four degrees up and eighteen degrees down. The tail incidence gear was operated via cables, the tailplane rear spar being moved between one and seven degrees by means of an elevating tube at the fuselage sternpost.

A Vickers 0.303in machine-gun with single CC synchronising gear Type C was fitted inside the port side of the fuselage, firing along a steel blast channel let into the fuselage side. The body of the gun was covered by a fairing panel that was humped to clear the gun projections and slotted to pass the cartridge and link chutes. Its cocking lever was accessible from the pilot's seat, and up to 600 rounds of ammunition were housed in a transverse metal box beneath the pilot's feet. Aiming was by ring-and-bead sight on the fuselage top decking, and the trigger was in the control column handle.

The pilot's aluminium seat in Bay 3 had a padded backrest and was designed to take a seat-type parachute. It incorporated a ratchet mechanism that could be operated without the pilot leaving the seat, allowing a vertical adjustment of four inches. The throttle and altitude controls for the engine were operated by levers in a quadrant on the port side of the cockpit.

At the centre of the instrument panel were the airspeed indicator, altimeter and revolution counter, and above these were the watch and oil temperature gauges. To the left side were the tail incidence and wing camber indicators, and the main engine switch was on the extreme left. On the right were the inclinometer, starting magneto switch and various oil and water pressure and temperature gauges. In a recessed portion of the panel in front of the control column were the fuel contents gauge, the dashboard and main electric switch boxes and, if wingtip flares were fitted, the two switches for their ignition. Below and in front of the pilot's knees was the compass. There was provision for a Gosport speaking tube with mouth- and earpieces. When fitted, the tube passed along the starboard side of the fuselage from the pilot's cockpit to the rear of the gun cockpit. The flexible tubing was secured by clips under the top fairing.

The pilot's canvas map case was affixed to the starboard side of the cockpit, and a fire extinguisher was stowed in spring clips to his right. Three high-pressure oxygen cylinders could be installed beneath the pilot's seat.

In the rear cockpit, on the port side of the lower portion of the metal partition dividing it from the pilot's cockpit, were mounted an airspeed indicator,

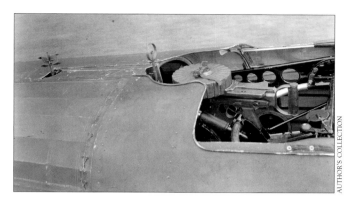

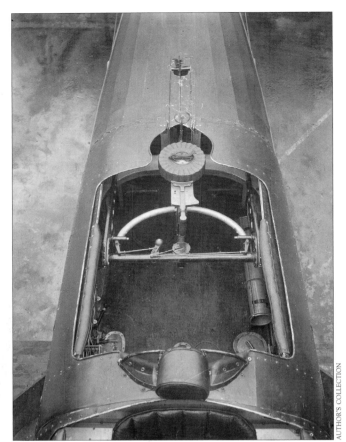

AUTHOR'S COLLECTION

AUTHOR'S COLLECTION

an altimeter and a watch, positioned where they could easily be read when the occupant was in a prone position for sighting or bomb dropping. The course-setting bombsight Mk IIB or VI was mounted on the side of the trap door opening, the door hinging back and attaching to the bulkhead. A sliding panel in the fuselage fairing was then slid back.

The rear cockpit occupied Bays 4 and 5. The observer's collapsible seat was hinged to fold against the port side of the fuselage to permit freedom of movement. His Lewis gun could be mounted either on a Scarff ring No 7 or on a Fairey high-speed gun mounting which allowed the gun to be stowed in the rear top decking when not in use. Ammunition was carried in six Mk II No 2 magazines, each holding 97 rounds. Five were located on pegs in the rear cockpit, four on the port side and one on the front bulkhead; the other was on the gun.

Three optional bomb loads could be carried on underwing racks: two 230-pound or 250-pound high-explosive (HE) and four 20-pound HE bombs; four 112-pound HE and four 20-pound HE bombs; or sixteen 20-pound HE bombs. In the first two instances the larger bombs were carried under the inner bays and the 20-pound sighter bombs under the outer bay on the port side. Bomb release could be controlled from either cockpit using the same type of release gear: the pilot's release was on the starboard side of his seat, while the observer's was on the starboard side of the bombing aperture. Selective, salvo and light series release could be selected.

A P.7 camera could be carried in fuselage Bay 6, the starboard portion of the floor being removed when the camera was to be used. It was operated by a release lever on the port side of the rear cockpit near the observer's seat. There was provision for a G.3 camera gun to be fitted on top of the starboard bottom mainplane. The wireless transmitter and receiver were located in Bay 5. They lay along the starboard side of the fuselage when not in use, and could be swung into position diagonally across the fuselage for operation from the observer's seat. A

Above, left: The rear cockpit of the two-seat general-purpose version, with the Lewis gun on the Fairey mounting stowed. Above, right: The rear cockpits of the three-seat general-purpose IIIF.

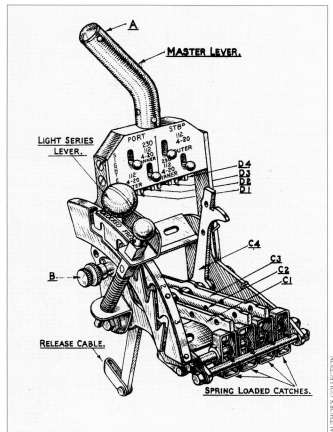

MASTER LEVER.

LIGHT SERIES
LEVER.

PORT   STBD
230   112
112   4·20
4·20   OUTER
INNER   230
        112
112   4·20
4·20   INNER
OUTER

D4
D3
D2
D1

C4
C3
C2
C1

B

RELEASE CABLE.

SPRING LOADED CATCHES.

AUTHOR'S COLLECTION

AUTHOR'S COLLECTION

1,200-volt generator was driven by a windmill which could be swung out of the starboard side of the fuselage into the slipstream. A 300-foot aerial wire was wound on a reel on the starboard side of Bay 4.

For desert operations, special boxes for rations and medical supplies, a five-gallon water container, tool kits and the crew's personal kit could be carried, and a spare wheel could be fitted under the fuselage.

The IIIF could be adapted to serve as an ambulance by removing the gun mounting and the hooding over the rear cockpit, enabling a standard Army

Above, left: The view through the underfuselage trapdoor for bomb-aiming.
Above, right: A drawing showing the bomb release lever.

Left: Stowage of a spare wheel between the undercarriage legs of the general-purpose IIIF.

AUTHOR'S COLLECTION

Left: Both the RAF and FAA variants of the IIIF could accommodate a standard Army stretcher, special gear having been designed to enable a loaded stretcher to be put in place and removed without excessive tilting. No conversion or alteration whatsoever was required, all fittings necessary for placing and holding the stretcher in position being permanently installed in the aircraft. Only the hooding around the cockpits needed to be removed, and cowling clips made this readily detachable.

stretcher to be accommodated. The hooding was then replaced. A standard machine could be converted and a loaded stretcher installed within five minutes. The head end of the stretcher was fastened by a wedge plate on the floor of fuselage Bay 3, while the foot end was held by two brackets at the rear edge of the floor panel in Bay 7. The aircraft could be converted into a dual-control trainer by removing the equipment in the rear cockpit and installing a DC conversion set and a special cowling.

In the three-seat FAA variant the observer's map case was fitted on the underside of the chart board, which was detachable and hinged at the top with two vertical struts fitted to the side of the observer's cockpit. When in use it was swung down to rest on his lap. The chart board was removed when the camera was carried, as the latter was mounted on the vertical struts. A signal pistol Mk I

Below: A view showing the accessibility of the Napier Lion with all cowling removed.

was stowed in a green Willesden canvas holster below the hoop stiffener at the front of the observer's cockpit. Eight cartridges were stowed in a pouch below his instrument panel. The signalling lamp was housed in a felt-lined 'registering base' fitted to starboard on the flooring to the telegraphist air gunner's cockpit. The shade for the lamp was stowed on the underside of the observer's seat. Signal flares were stowed under the fairing within the top rear portion of the fuselage, within reach from the rear cockpit, and four aluminium-powder sea markers were stowed in the spares box at the back of the observer's cockpit. The crew had safety belts secured to the fuselage by cable and eyebolts. In the telegraphist air gunner's case, provision was made for anchoring his harness by means of an eye-plate fitting

Above: The pre-production IIIF Mk I S1147 (c/n F888), complete with underwing bombs, shows the configuration of the general-purpose version.
Below: The same machine with all cowling and hooding removed to show accessibility—a three-minute operation.

51

secured to the cockpit floor. Irvin parachutes were provided, seat types for the pilot and observer and a detachable type for the TAG.

Additional equipment was fitted for shipborne operations. Holding-down gear was employed for stowage on a deck catapult. This included wing fittings permanently attached to the spars in the region of the interplane strut joints; for interchangeability these were incorporated on all Fairey IIIF and Gordon aeroplanes. The aircraft was supported on the catapult and restrained by cables to the upper and lower planes and the floats. Steadying cables were attached to the front and rear fuselage. The restrain the ailerons and flaps from movement under 'stray air loads', jury struts were provided for fitting between the control surfaces of one wing and the rear spar of the other. Similar struts were provided for the rudder and elevators.

To keep the aircraft afloat in the event of a ditching, inflatable flotation bags were fitted. These comprised a pair of cylindrical rubberised fabric air bags each of 1,500-pounds' buoyancy attached to either side of the fuselage and stowed in compartments behind the side cowling. They were inflated when required by air contained in two bottles under the pilot's seat and were controlled by the pilot. A collapsible dinghy was stowed under the cowling on a tray clipped to the fuselage top longerons on Bays 8 and 9. The cowling was hinged along the starboard side of the fuselage and secured on the port side by two pins with a wire release that could be operated by either the pilot or observer. The dinghy was inflated by an electric blower immediately behind the tray and controlled by a switch on the cowling of the pilot's cockpit; a duplicate switch was provided for the observer. The cowling had to be released before the blower was switched on, but in any case the blower had to be operated before water reached either the batteries or the blower itself.

A lifting sling was fitted in the centre section of the upper wing. It consisted of four lengths of cable eye

Above: A photograph of the newly completed IIIF Mk I S1182 in 1927. This machine was destined to serve in both the RAF and the Fleet Air Arm, finally going to Driffield as at a 'test bench' after being deemed uneconomical to repair in December 1936.
Below: A front view of S1147 with its wings folded.

AUTHOR'S COLLECTION

spliced to the ends of the centre section's front and rear spars. The loose ends of the cables were brought together, the pyramid thus formed terminating in a triangular link that could be engaged in the hook of the lifting tackle. Another sling, called a 'pennant', was provided to pick up the main sling in the event of the forward portion of the aircraft being submerged. This sling was led from the front catapult fittings along the outside of the fuselage to the rear end, where it terminated in spliced eyes. The cables were fastened to the fuselage by long strips of fabric. When these cables were to be used, the eyes at the rear end of the fuselage were picked up and the cables ripped from the fabric strips. In this way the forward end of the aeroplane could be raised sufficiently to make the main sling available for the final hoist.

Above: Another view of Fairey IIIF Mk I S1182 in 1927. The forward-firing Vickers gun is not installed, and there is a standard Scarff ring on the rear cockpit.
Below: Another view of S1147 with its wings folded. Notice the jury strut at the inboard leading edge of the folded port wing, and also that used to raise the tail to keep the wing tips clear of the ground.

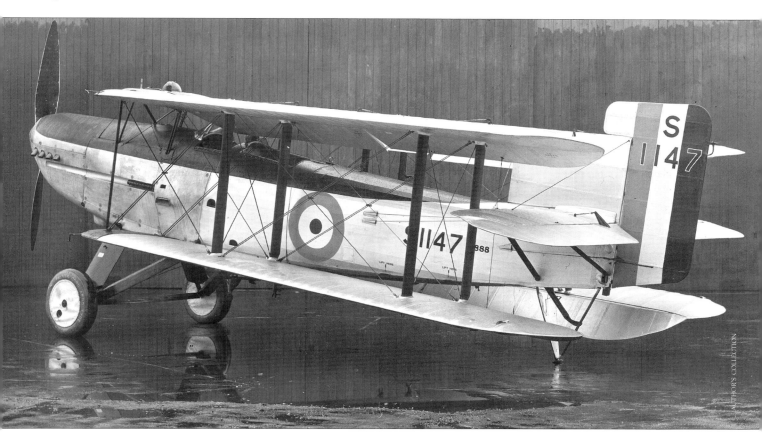

AUTHOR'S COLLECTION

53

Left, upper, and below: Representative of the Mk IVM/A with its all-metal airframe, J9640 served with No 45 Squadron in the Middle East from September 1929, being rebuilt as JR9640 in 1934.
Left, lower: Factory-fresh all-metal IIIF Mk IIIM S1320, powered by a 570hp Lion XIA, poses for the camera. This aircraft was destined for service in HMS Eagle.
Right: Newly completed IIIF Mk IVC (GP) J9068 shows off its elegant lines. This aircraft served with No 8 Squadron in Aden.

'No Outstanding Vices'

Flying the Fairey IIIF

PROBABLY the earliest 'Pilot's Notes' for flying the IIIF were contained in a loose-leaf maintenance manual for the type issued by Fairey Aviation in January 1927. Given the early date of this publication, the notes almost certainly refer to N198, the first prototype, and were doubtless compiled by Captain Norman Macmillan. They read as follows:

PILOT'S COCKPIT AND CONTROLS

The air [flying] controls consist of a control stick and adjustable rudder pedals. The tailplane adjusting gear is operated by means of a wheel on the port side of the cockpit. A wheel on the starboard side of the cockpit is the means of adjusting the flaps. Throttle and altitude control levers are mounted on a quadrant situated on the port side of the cockpit. The retractable radiator is raised and lowered by means of a crank handle mounted below the starboard side of the instrument board. On the instrument board are found the usual flying instruments, with the compass mounted in front of the control stick.

The front gun is mounted inside the cockpit on the lower port side.

The ignition switches are mounted on the instrument board, a separate single switch being employed for the starting magneto. The starting magneto is operated automatically when the starting handles are turned.

THE FUEL SYSTEM. From the sump of the lower of the interconnected fuel tanks, a single pipe line runs through the filter to the shut-off cock and hand pump in the cockpit, thence to the engine pump relief valve and carburetters. There is only one cock to which the pilot need attend. This cock is "ON" when the handle is in line with the pipe, and "OFF" when at right angles to it. When at

Below and opposite, bottom: A pre-production IIIF Mk I, S1148 (the same aircraft later used for seaplane deck-landing trials), displays its agility for the photographer. Of incidental interest are the Bessoneau portable hangars in the background of the side view, and the 'leaning' of the buildings in the image of the aircraft banking, caused by the focal plane shutter as the camera was panned to follow the aircraft.

rest — that is before starting up, fuel must be supplied by the hand pump. The fuel pressure is registered by a gauge fitted to the instrument board. There is no gravity tank. If the engine petrol pump fails, the hand pump can be used instantly without changing the position of the cock.

Above: The pre-production Fairey IIIF Mk I two-seater S1147 at Martlesham Heath in March 1927, with bombs underwing. The RAE used this machine for spinning tests in 1929.

THE FAIREY-REED AIRSCREW

The engine must NEVER BE TURNED by grasping the airscrew blade tips. Use the starting handles or, if absolutely necessary, PULL FROM THE THICK CENTRE PART OF THE AIRSCREW BLADE INSIDE THE RED LINES. When the aircraft is at rest the blades should be protected from accidental damage by fitting the gloves provided for this purpose.

TO START ENGINE

TO START ENGINE proceed as follows:—
1. Position aircraft head to wind; see that there is nothing on the ground which can be sucked up by the airscrew.
2. Chock wheels.
3. Turn on petrol, and give a few strokes with the hand pump.
4. See that switches are OFF.
5. Close throttle.
6. Give half a dozen charges with priming pump while mechanics turn engine starting handles to suck in.
7. Open throttle ¼"
8. Switch on, and continue turning starting handle.
Engine should now start.

WHEN STARTED
1. Run at 600rpm to warm up, with control radiator right up.
2. Check that,
   (a) Oil pressure is registering on gauge.
   (b) Petrol pressure is registering on gauge (about 2lb throttled down).
   (c) The retractable radiator is right UP.
   (d) Priming pump cock is OFF.

WHEN WATER TEMPERATURE HAS REACHED 70°C. AND OIL TEMPERATURE 30° TO 40°,
1. Wind radiator fully down.
2. See that two men are on the tail. The best position is facing back over tailplane.
3. Open throttle only long enough to get a steady reading.
It is unnecessary to open out beyond 1,900rpm on the ground to test engine.

CHECK THAT:—
   (a) Engine turns at 1,900rpm. (The airscrew permits 2,020).

(b) Oil pressure is not less than 60lb per sq. inch at full throttle.

(c) Petrol pressure is not less than 2lb per sq. inch at full throttle.

(d) Each magneto fires evenly. The drop with either magneto cut out must not be more than 80rpm. Not more than 20rpm is the usual drop.

(e) Altitude control reduces the rpm.

TO STOP ENGINE

1. Turn off petrol.
2. Allow engine to run until the petrol in the piping is exhausted.
3. SWITCH OFF.
4. Wind retractable radiator right in to prevent damage.

TAXYING

The 3F [sic] is very stable when taxying, and does not require steadying in side winds. Avoid stones, dust, and cinders which may burr the airscrew tips.

BEFORE TAKING OFF

CHECK THAT:—

1. Water temperature is about 75°C.
2. The tailplane setting is 4°.
3. Flaps are set at 8° down.
4. Retractable radiator is full out in hot weather.
5. Oil pressure is recording. At slow engine speeds it will show about 40lb, at full throttle about 60lb to 70lb.
6. Petrol pressure is recording. At slow speeds about 2lb, at high speeds about 2 to 4lb.
7. Rudder pedal adjusting screws are tight. Rudder, ailerons and elevators are free over their full range of movement.
8. Petrol cock is in line with pip line, dope pump cock is OFF.
9. Ignition switch is on to both magnetos.

TAKING OFF

While opening the throttle hold the stick forward to lift the tail. Do not accelerate the engine violently.

Keep the tail up to maintain the fuselage in nearly level flying position while the aircraft accelerates. Before flying speed has been reached the aircraft will assume this attitude with the stick neutral. When flying speed has been reached (with full load and flaps normal at 52 knots, flaps 8° at 48 knots, flaps 12° at 47 knots) a slight backward movement of the stick will take her off. A little practice will enable the pilot to graduate the backward movement of the stick to a nicety so that the take off is smooth and progressive. The 3F does not swing taking off, and the take off is easy.

When carrying full load never take off without setting the tail plane to approximately 4° with 8° flaps. When flaps are set to normal move tail plane incidence slightly if required.

NORMAL FLIGHT

At equal speeds the 3F controls are lighter to operate than those on the normal two-seater fighter.

The tail plane adjustment covers the full speed range, engine on and off, and it should be trimmed to enable the aircraft to fly hands off. The amount of throttle used alters the fore and aft trim of the aircraft and the tailplane should be adjusted to suit.

CRUISING. The best cruising speed is about 100 knots at about 1,800/1,900rpm. This speed is indicated correctly on the ASI [airspeed indicator] at sea level, but at height indicated speed falls off with reduced density. This fall off for standard conditions of temperature and pressure is as follows:—

FOR EXAMPLE:—

Height	True Cruising Speed	ASI Registers
Sea level	125mph	
10,000ft	125mph	107mph
15,000ft	125mph	99mph

These figures do not take into account instrument or pitot position corrections.

At frequent intervals the pilot should check the water and oil temperatures, oil pressure, and petrol pressure. The retractable radiator should be adjusted to maintain a correct and steady water temperature.

CLIMBING FLIGHT

Before leaving the ground the radiator must be set out, and adjusted as required during climb.

CLIMBING SPEED. Off the ground the best climbing speed, with full load, is 68 knots. A reduction in indicated speed of 1 knot per 2,000ft is required to maintain maximum climb to ceiling. Drag should be reduced to the minimum by setting the tail plane so that there is no load on the stick. Flaps should be set at 4° down after taking off, and gradually lowered as the climb continues to a maximum of 10° down at about 15,000.

To achieve the maximum rate of climb it is important that the indicated speed remain steady throughout the climb. Any surging of the needle up and down the scale, due to bumps or the pilot's hands, will decrease the rate of climb.

ENGINE SYMPTOMS DURING CLIMB. During the climb the pilot should note his engine revolutions. The drop in revolutions should be very gradual and must not be excessive. Any pronounced drop indicates too slow climbing speed, misuse or neglect of altitude control, or engine defect. Before deciding that the engine is at fault the pilot should determine that,

(a) He is climbing at the correct indicated speed for the indicated altitude.
(b) That the carburation [sic] is properly controlled on the altitude control.
(c) That the water temperature is correct.
(d) That the oil pressure is not below 60lb per sq inch.
(e) That the petrol pressure is correct.
(f) Each magneto is firing evenly, by testing on switch.

Above: Both the early and later fin and rudder designs are evident in this gunner's-eye view from the inside of a formation of IIIFs of No 207 Squadron RAF over Hendon in June 1928, rehearsing for the 1928 Royal Air Force Display. The nearest machine, J9136/ 'A1', was a IIIF Mk IVC/M; beneath its tail is S1182/'A3', a Mk I that later went into FAA service, and beyond its under-carriage is J9057/'C1', a Mk IVC (GP). The aircraft in the far distance above S1182's tail is a Hawker Horsley.

AUTHOR'S COLLECTION

59

WATER TEMPERATURE CONTROL WITH VARYING ALTITUDES

At sea level the water boils at			100°C
At 5,000ft	"	"	95°
At 10,000ft	"	"	90°
At 15,000ft	"	"	85°
At 20,000ft	"	"	80°

The outlet water temperature must be regulated accordingly.
At moderate altitudes the best outlet temperature is 75°C. At height careful watch must be kept that the water temperature does not creep up as the boiling point comes down.

It should be remembered that if a pilot can handle his craft well in a climb, and obtain maximum rate of climb and ceiling, he knows his machine and shows skill in using it.

LANDING

The aircraft is very easy to land, but the pilot must remember that lowering the flaps increases the relative wing angle to the fuselage, and this must be allowed for when flattening out, because of the alteration in relative angle thus produced between the aircraft fuselage and the ground. When this is remembered flaps can be utilised to full advantage. The landing speeds are as for take off but the aircraft should be glided in 10 knots faster.

In 1929 the RAE undertook spinning tests using IIIF Mk I S1147. This machine had originally been modified as the two-seat general-purpose prototype for the RAF, but the RAE re-modified it to ensure that the loadings corresponded with those of the FAA version. Spins were entered at an altitude of 11,000 feet, and eight to twelve turns were made before recovery. Although there was no difficulty in recovering from a spin with the CG positions near the aft limit and flap settings between zero and 15 degrees, there was pronounced jerkiness in the rotation, with marked pitch oscillations. The aircraft recovered, at an indicated air speed of 110 to 130mph, at a very steep attitude. However, the IIIF certainly had some undesirable spinning characteristics, even in its landplane form, and several accidents in service were attributed to a failure to recover from a flat spin.

In 1932 similar tests were made at the RAE using Mk IIIM S1317. This time, lead-shot ballast simulated the aft CG and increased the inertia effects of the arrester hook being fitted to deck-landing IIIFs, which weighed 45 pounds. Prolonged spins to the right were slow and uneven, and 1,000 feet was lost in recovery. Spins to the left were considerably flatter, with a height loss in recovery of up to 1,500 feet. With full fuel tanks, recovery from a left-hand spin was described as 'by no means rapid'.

Before this, on 5 January 1931, Flight Sergeant Herbert Victor Hudson of No 207 Squadron RAF at Bircham Newton, Norfolk, had set out from the base in IIIF Mk IVC/M J9137/'B2' with Leading Aircraftman C. H. Molyneux as his air gunner. In the account he sent to the Irvin Air Chute Company he recalled that

At 3,800 feet over Bircham I dived the machine and lifted her in a climbing turn to gain the last 300 feet and come back on my first course. Shortly after this turn commenced the machine shuddered, dropped her right wing violently and the nose sank quietly. I attempted to correct as far as a normal spin, but this only accentuated the trouble and so I lifted the nose as high as possible and throttled back. With full throttle the machine spun violently to the right.

With full throttle and stick back and to the left—also with full left rudder—the machine remained spinning steadily to the right, right wing down about 30 degrees, and dropping steadily, further down, nose being just on the horizon and losing height rapidly.

I ordered Molyneux to jump, and after some difficulty and delay—he was using the new [Irvin] Quick Connector Air Chute—he climbed over the side. The loose pack slipped out of his hands and caught up in the Scarff gun-mounting, and he had some difficulty in clearing it, but at last managed to do so. He remained

Right: The addition of Handley Page slots (also referred to as 'slats') on the outer leading edges of the upper wing improved lateral stability near the stall, but, although they made it harder to enter a stall, the spin was faster with slots, and test pilot Captain Norman Macmillan found that the aircraft spun with one slot open and one closed. Moreover, recovery was harder and 'a good deal slower'. The port slot is conspicuous in this shot of IIIF Mk IV J9655 of 'B' Flight, No 45 Squadron, over the Nile near Wadi Halfa in 1930, piloted by Sergeant Tomkins. Note also the fully extended radiator, the spare wheel between the main under-carriage legs and the flare brackets beneath the lower wingtips.

Right: The wreckage of Fairey IIIF Mk IVC/M J9137 after it entered an irrecoverable spin on 5 January 1931 and crashed at Heacham in Norfolk. Its crew, pilot Flight Sergeant H. V. Hudson and gunner Leading Aircraftman C. H. Molyneaux, baled out safely, the latter becoming the first person to save his life using the new Irvin Quick Connector Air Chute. Both men and the aircraft came to earth within a thirty-yard radius.

hanging on the side, all clear, and so, as the height indicator then showed 1,800 feet (and the machine would, of course, suffer from 'lag', falling so quickly), I saw there was no time to waste. Having cast off my belt and speaking tubes, while waiting for him, I stood up in my seat, released the stick, and as the machine was now released from my check it shot over the right and plunged downwards.

I dived on top of Molyneux and we both went clear almost together. I delayed ripping to get clear of him and suddenly saw the machine close to me, but whether above, below or beside me I do not know, save that it was in front of me, so I waited a further period of time, which I am quite unable to estimate.

At last, seeing as I turned over and over the ground perilously close, I ripped the cord. Immediately it seemed I was pulled up quickly and upright, not hurt, but seized as in a strong hand. My fall was arrested. Simultaneously, I saw a garden beneath me and I almost at once dropped amongst cabbages.

I do not remember feeling any jar, but just making firm impact. As I rolled over on my back I saw the other parachute falling about 50 yards away. Thanks to your wonderful Air Chutes, Molyneux [the first man to jump for his life with a Quick Connector Chute] also escaped without even a very heavy jar on landing. He ripped almost immediately on leaving the machine and his parachute opened instantly, letting him down gently in what he says was an extremely pleasant manner to the ground.

He thoroughly enjoyed it. From the reports of my eye-witnesses, amongst whom were two who were competent to judge, it would appear that my chute opened about 50 feet from the ground, yet I felt no heavy jar or shock.

A remarkable thing about it all was that from the second of failure I had not the least fear of the Irvin failing me, and my confidence was well founded. On casting back my mind I can recall no period of time whatsoever from the time I pulled the rip cord till I felt myself swing upright in my harness.

The observer, like myself, hit first on his feet and then rolled on his back. He landed on harder ground and received a rather severe bump on his buttocks, but was none the worse for it. Neither of us had previously made a practice jump. We are, needless to say, warm in praise of the Irvin Air Chute, and certainly I should never feel happy in the air without one. It would need to be a matter of great urgency which would cause me to fly without my Irvin in future, if indeed, I should ever be persuaded to do so.

Like the mariners who say 'Thank God for Plimsoll', I feel like saying 'Thank God for Irving [sic]'.

P.S. The machine was utterly wrecked and, but for our Irvins, there is not the slightest doubt that we should have been killed outright. Pilot, Air Gunner and machine all ended up in Heacham, Norfolk, within 30 yards of one another.

On 18 May 1931 an RAF Fairey IIIF had been involved in what the Irvin Air Chute Company subsequently described as 'one of the most remarkable escapes in the history of parachuting'. Sergeant Pilot D. J. Pitcher, serving with No 45 Squadron in Egypt, had been detailed to fly to Ismailia in IIIF Mk IVM/A J9662. On the return journey he had Leading Aircraftman W. R. Fraser, the machine's fitter, as his passenger, and on arriving over Helwan at about 1700 hours he decided to carry out a few aerobatics as the aircraft was comparatively light. Commencing from a height of 4,200 feet, he performed two loops in succession, followed by a stall-turn to the right, dropping as intended into a spin to the right, this spin beginning at 3,200 feet. Pitcher's intention was to make two complete turns and then resume normal flight and land, but when he checked the spin in the normal manner the IIIF's nose came up well above the spinning axis and the manœuvre developed into a 'decided flat spin'. While the aircraft was thus spinning, its nose oscillated from the horizontal to approximately 45 degrees below.

Left: All-metal Mk IIIM S1393 displays the later exhaust system from the starboard side, with an additional upper pipe for the four cylinders in the vertical top row. This picture was probably taken at the School of Naval Co-operation at Lee-on-Solent in 1936–37, as the tail of Blackburn Shark K5636, which was serving there at the same time as S1393, is visible on the right.

Left: This pair of IIIF Mk IIIB seaplanes of the Training Flight of the School of Naval Co-operation at Lee-on-Solent, S1521/'Z' and S1502/'D', display the curved exhaust pipes later fitted to many IIIFs to direct the Lion's hot and toxic exhaust gases well clear of structure and crew. Both machines lack propeller spinners.

Pitcher had more than 500 hours on IIIFs and had spun them 'as a regular thing', but he had never encountered such behaviour before, nor experienced any difficulty in recovering from spins. (No defect was found in the aircraft by the subsequent Court of Inquiry.) Although he did his utmost to recover from the position, even using both hands on the control column and finally trying a burst of engine, nothing he did altered the course of the aircraft in the slightest. Realising that it was more or less impossible to recover in the remaining height, Pitcher told Fraser to jump, and he attempted to leave on his nearest side, the left, which happened to be on the outside of the spin. Fraser found this impossible and promptly left by the right-hand side, finding it necessary to use both hands to push himself away from the aircraft. Once clear, he had no difficulty in finding the ripcord ring.

Deciding to jump at what could have been no more than 800 feet, Pitcher undid his safety belt, raised himself by pulling on the windscreen, and sat on the right-hand side of the fuselage, legs inside, parachute outside. In that position he looked for the ring and grasped it, thinking there was very little height to spare. He must have pulled the ring while still in contact with the machine, and the main parachute opened almost instantaneously. This seemed strange to him at the time, but seeing Fraser just below him, and with his parachute in order and he himself quite safe (a 'wonderful feeling'), he did not give this much thought. He later said that he was exceptionally fortunate in that respect, because apparently

Below: Fairey IIIF Mk II S1312, strengthened for catapulting, is seen here during its period as No 46 of 447 Flight, serving in HMS *Sussex* with the First Cruiser Squadron in the Mediterranean, probably in the latter half of 1931.

his pulling off so near the machine caused the pilot 'chute to open instantly and it was blown into the tailskid. The tailplane struck Pitcher across the legs when he was falling inverted and, the pilot 'chute being caught up and he being at the mercy of 'man-gravity', the main parachute opened before he was a dozen feet from the aircraft. However, he felt no shock on the harness. The main and pilot parachutes parted at the pilot 'chute rigging lines, the pilot 'chute being left on the IIIF's tailskid. The main parachute was not affected in the least, and Pitcher was using it, after repairs and inspection, three days later.

Pitcher thought that the two parachutes reached the ground within twelve seconds of taking effect, about twenty yards apart. Fraser landed to windward and both men were unhurt, though Fraser found it uncomfortable to sit down for a few days as he had unfortunately alighted facing the wind, which was blowing at 10mph. The IIIF crashed about seventy yards away to windward. Pitcher said that, in both of their views, their experiences proved beyond a shadow of doubt that the Irvin parachute was exceedingly quick and efficient. Both men felt it was their duty to write to Irvin expressing their gratitude. They were the first members in No 45 Squadron's history to make parachute descents.

On 23 May 1932 Leading Aircraftman Leslie Charles Menet saved his life by baling out of a IIIF of No 14 (Bomber) Squadron piloted by Flying Officer Eric Victor Newcomen Bramley and also carrying Leading Aircraftman Gerald William Moore, both of whom were killed. They were on their way back from Aboukir and had left Heliopolis for Amman at 10 a.m. Four miles north-east of Gaza in Palestine things started to go wrong, as Menet recounted:

I was laying [sic] down in the rear of the cockpit with my eyes closed, endeavouring to doze a little. Luckily I was wearing my own observer type chute and all buckles were done up. The first incident that put me on the qui vive was the throttling back of the engine, followed by a smell of burning rubber, possibly caused by an electrical fuse in the front cockpit. The pilot decided to turn back

Below: Two IIIF Mk IIIBs of the School of Naval Co-operation go about their business at Lee-on-Solent. Nearest is S1520/'Y', and taxying in the distance is S1521/'Z'. The ground crew on the left are taking away S1520's float trolley wheels. Taxying, take-offs and landings in the sea-plane demanded very different techniques from those needed for the landplane—as pilots quickly discovered.

Left, upper and lower: The wreckage of IIIF Mk IVM/A J9662 of No 45 Squadron RAF after it entered an irrecoverable flat spin while its pilot, Sergeant Pilot D. J. Pitcher, was performing aerobatics over Helwan, Egypt, on 18 May 1931. Pitcher and his passenger, leading Aircraftman W. R. Fraser, baled out, thereby becoming the first Squadron members ever to make parachute descents.

and land at Gaza aerodrome. In executing a left-hand turn the machine stalled and went down in a right-hand spin. The pilot prepared to leave the machine and I took up my position in the rear of the cockpit with my back half turned towards the remainder of the crew. I had one foot dug in the side of the cockpit, steadying myself with the right hand on the fuselage. I was prepared to leave the machine when it was half-way through the second turn, but I waited the start of the third turn and dived off head first from the starboard side of the aircraft.

I did not count, but judged when I considered I was clear of aircraft. On pulling rip cord parachute opened immediately, and I suffered no shock; in fact I liken the experience to the end of a lift descent. I immediately looked for my companions, and I was horror-struck to see that they had not left the machine.

The spin of the machine had increased in speed and the other two occupants left just before it hit the ground. I saw the whites of pilot parachutes appear. I was about 1,000 feet up when I left the machine and I landed 100 yards from it without sustaining any injury, although I was only wearing tennis shoes. I ran towards my companions and covered them up with their chutes, which had just started to unfold.

I believe that if they had jumped two seconds earlier they would have saved their lives. My parachute was inspected and repacked and I still have it in my charge.

The aircraft crashed two miles north of Gaza.

The floatplane version's spinning characteristics were worse. One MAEE crew, pilot Flight Lieutenant A. G. Pickering and scientific officer/observer Mr A. Woodward Nutt, were obliged to abandon IIIF Mk IIIM S1316 on 13 June 1931 when it entered a flat spin to the left from which it refused to recover during spinning tests with autoslots at an all-up weight of 5,895 pounds and the c.g. aft. According to his own account, Pickering climbed the machine to 7,400 feet, then started to spin with the intention of doing only two or three turns. He had great difficulty in getting the stick forward, but managed it with all his strength. With the stick right forward and opposite rudder, the seaplane still spun with no sign of coming out. When they were down to 3,000 feet Pickering told his passenger to jump, and at 2,000 feet he followed him over the side. Both Irvin parachutes

COURTESY TIM MASON

opened at once and landed them without a scratch, Pickering in an oak tree and Woodward Nutt in the middle of a field. The wind at the time was only 3mph.

In a letter of application for membership of the Caterpillar Club, which is exclusive to those who have saved their lives by the use of Irvin Airchutes, Woodward Nutt wrote:

> I was flying as observer in a Fairey IIIF seaplane in order to take observations during experimental spins.
>
> Flight Lieut. Pickering was the pilot. During the first spin we attempted, Pickering shouted to me after he had made several turns to the effect that the seaplane was not answering the controls properly, and soon after he signalled me to jump.
>
> I signified that I understood and got ready to leave. I then waited until I saw him jump clear over the left-hand side of the machine and then prepared to follow suit.
>
> I found, however, that I could not get my foot on to the edge of the cockpit coaming owing to the fact that I was wearing a lap type parachute and the seat

Above: Another victim of the dreaded irrecoverable flat spin was IIIF Mk IIIM seaplane S1316, which ended up in this unfortunate state on 13 June 1931, during spinning tests with autoslots at the MAEE. Both its pilot, Flight Lieutenant A. G. Pickering, and civilian scientific officer/observer Mr A. Woodward Nutt baled out and escaped unhurt, even though Pickering ended up in an oak tree. The aircraft was apparently rebuilt and continued to serve.

AUTHOR'S COLLECTION

was very low relative to the coaming. I therefore stood on the seat and, holding up my pack with both hands, I faced the inside of the spin and jumped upwards as hard as I could.

I hoped to be able to kick myself clear, but my left foot struck the underside of the cockpit coaming and as my body pitched forward I pulled the ring, kicking hard at the same moment.

I have a recollection of feeling that the aeroplane was all round me for an instant, and of seeing the white flash of the opening parachute. I was expecting to be hit by some part of the aeroplane, but fortunately was not, and my next recollection is of finding myself supported, a little breathless, comparatively motionless in space, while the aeroplane fell rapidly away.

The silence and apparent lack of movement, except for a rather pleasant swinging, were very noticeable after the rush and roar of the seaplane. I was greatly impressed by the rapidity with which the parachute opened, and by the fact that I felt no sudden shock when it did.

It was a clear sunny day and I had a splendid view of the countryside from my comparatively high altitude. I saw the seaplane spinning downwards, and almost immediately the rotation suddenly stopped and it seemed to crumple up. The sound of a hollow crash came up to me. I then saw Pickering's parachute a little way below me and shouted to him. I heard his answering shout and then he suddenly landed in the top of a tree. I saw that I was over green fields, but was drifting towards a fence and some trees, so I pulled hard on what I hoped were the right shrouds. There was no apparent effect, but the fields suddenly came up to meet me at what seemed an enormous speed. I had just time to let myself go limp before I landed and rolled over.

I got up immediately and saw the parachute collapsing. There was practically no wind and I had fallen on soft springy turf. I undid the harness and ran over to help Pickering out of his tree. I was glad to find that he was unhurt. We then walked over to see our wrecked seaplane about 300 to 400 yards away.

Owing to patches of cloud and the position of the altimeter in the aircraft we were uncertain of the exact height at which we jumped, but from the records retrieved from the wreck it seems that we left between 2,500 and 3,000 feet. The seaplane struck the ground about 22 seconds afterwards.

Both men were granted Caterpillar Club membership, but it is interesting to note the conspicuous discrepancy in the two accounts as to who left the aeroplane first! The surprising thing is that, although Woodward Nutt described the crashed S1316 as a 'wreck', it appears to have survived, as it is recorded as going to RAE Farnborough 'for catapult course' on 5 November 1931.

As a result of this episode, Service crews were advised to follow the example set by Pickering and Woodward Nutt should spin develop or continue below 1,500 feet.

As far as the IIIF's general handling was concerned, test pilot Captain Norman Macmillan recalled:

Above: 'Find a clear run of at least a mile'; IIIF Mk IIIM S1386 of No 202 Squadron begins its take-off run at Calafrana, Malta. Left to its own devices, the seaplane would 'plough along fussily in a cloud of spray at about 30 knots' indefinitely if the pilot took no further action. This aircraft was deemed beyond economical repair after it was hit by Fairey Swordfish K5943 of 825 Squadron while taxying at Hal Far on 10 October 1936.

Opposite, bottom: A pilot of No 202 (Flying Boat) Squadron gets a piggy-back to shore after bringing IIIF Mk IIIB S1525 to the slipway at Calafrana, Malta. Depending on whether the wind was favourable or otherwise, beaching of the aircraft after a flight could be 'exciting' and required a knowledge of seamanship as well as flying.

All her controls were powerful, and although [the wings] had no stagger [to allow the wings to be folded], her longitudinal stability was excellent owing to her long fuselage moment with ample tail and elevator surfaces. She carried rudder in flight and this could not be trimmed as no trimmer was fitted; yet I had no difficulty in leaving Northolt one day in London fog and cloud, and climbing up through the murk without blind flying instruments.

I liked the Lion V; it was freer from vibration than the later uprated Lions, and it ran very smoothly with the Fairey-Reed metal propeller.

She was easy to fly as a floatplane, with excellent water stability and good control even in quite strong winds. Take-off from the water was easy, almost but not quite automatic from the hydroplaning condition, only a slight rear pressure on the controls needed to unstick.

Aerobatically the IIIF landplane was surprisingly good. She looped with ease. She spun fast, with swift entry when deliberately stalled and ruddered, but she recovered quickly. Floatplane spins were different and at least 1,500 feet altitude above the sea were needed in which to recover level flight.

When IIIFs were later fitted with Handley Page slots, I found that flight near the stall possessed improved lateral stability, but I also found that it was still possible to spin the landplane, although entry was more difficult. When she did spin, she spun even faster with slots and I found that she spun with one slot open and the other closed. It was more difficult to recover from a spin when slots were fitted; more control had to be applied and the recovery was a good deal slower.

Negative flap gave slightly faster speed when flying full out level, chiefly because it altered the fuselage angle slightly, and probably reduced the drag due to the open rear cockpits. Minus 2 degrees flap was best for top speed, plus 4 degrees for take-off and plus 8 for landing.

The Lion was generally noted for its reliability, but on 2 January 1929 Macmillan experienced an in-flight failure, an incident he describes vividly in *Wings of Fate* (London: G. Bell & Sons Ltd, 1967). He had flown in a IIIF from Northolt to RAF Cranwell with George Pate, Napier's chief engineer, as a passenger. Their task was to make test flight of the Fairey Long Range ('Postal') Monoplane, but before their departure Pate had expressed concern about the number of Lions being returned to the works in a damaged state for repair.

Having completed the tests, late in the afternoon Macmillan and Pate took off in the IIIF for the return flight. The aircraft, which was the RAF machine in which Macmillan had flown special consumption tests of the Lion XI for comparison with the Rolls-Royce F.12B in a D.H.9A, had no navigation lights, but there was just enough time to reach Northolt before dark. They were flying

Below: This is almost certainly S1479/'45', a IIIF Mk IIIB of 440 Flight, taking off from HMS *Hermes*. Note the smokestream wind indicator and the windbreak folded down flat on the deck.

smoothly in the calm and windless air over Lincolnshire at 1,000 feet, some ten miles from Cranfield, when, as Macmillan recalled, 'Suddenly a violent percussion interrupted the sweet running of the engine. It came without warning, followed instantly by repetitive hammering of metal on metal under the engine cowling. Revs dropped. The framework of the IIIF shuddered.'

Macmillan's instinctive test-pilot reactions were triggered with the first sound. He instantly 'shut the throttle, switched off, banked hard left, pushed the left rudder pedal to bring the nose down, and hauled back on the stick, losing not a second in entering that tight gliding turn, for both time and distance were too precious to be lost'. He had seen a reasonably sized field, bordered by a stone wall, just before the trouble started, and, straightening out on the reciprocal of that field, he stretched his glide to the maximum. The propeller stopped and the metallic clanking ceased, but Macmillan concentrated on the challenge ahead. As he approached the field he judged he could reach the boundary with 'a mere handful of height to spare'. He continues:

> To use the flaps too soon would steepen the glide too much and bring [me] down short of the field. At the last critical moment [I] wound them down and reset the tail [incidence] to suit. Now [my] eyes focused exclusively on the stone wall [I] had to clear. It was about six feet high. With the mastery of the Gosport [training] system [I] held [my] glide straight and steady, safeguarding height to clear the wall. It came close. Side-slipping away [my] fraction of surplus height, [I] crossed it, watching [my] depressed wing's tip clear the stone by inches. [I] turned the nose again into the line of flight, levelled off and, softly, the IIIF sank to the ground, close to the wall. She had no brakes. [I] hoped no ditch cut the field. There was none. She stopped rolling and rested on a hard, smooth grazing surface. Now, tension relaxed, [I] felt [I] had never made a better forced landing when the glide odds were so very near the limit of the impossible.

After unclipping his belt and parachute harness, Macmillan climbed from the cockpit and ran round to the aircraft's nose. He saw the end of a connecting rod protruding from the Lion engine and poking out through a rent in the polished cowling. As he helped Pate down, the engineer remarked, 'Let me congratulate you on a wonderful landing. It was marvellous.'

When Macmillan showed Pate the cause of their forced landing, Pate said that when he got back to his office he would have to write about fifty letters apologising to the Service pilots he had condemned for not knowing beforehand that their engines were going to fail. He added that he never knew that anything was wrong until he felt himself being pressed hard into his seat when Macmillan rapidly turned back; he had not even heard the bang when the con-rod failed, or the subsequent hammering.

Macmillan had flown a little more than ten hours with the engine before its in-flight failure. A thorough investigation of this incident and the previous ones revealed that a connecting rod was always the part that failed first, and that it always failed at the crankpin end (this had also happened with the Rolls-Royce engine). Both failures had the same cause at their roots: during assembly, which was done by hand, the tightening of the nuts securing the big-end bearing caps depended on each fitter's individual judgement, and some tightened them more than others. This imposed an unnecessary load on the bolts or studs, adding to the load they had to bear when the engine was running. Consequently one and then another of the studs or bolts would break under the combined stress, and the remainder could not retain the bearing cap in position. When it came adrift the piston pushed the loose connecting rod down beyond its usual limit and the crankshaft hammered about inside the crankcase, which it often burst.

To eliminate the fitters' guesswork, the design staff calculated the correct tension for the bolts or studs and a torque spanner was devised which slipped at the design load, making it impossible for the nut to be tightened further. The connecting rod failures then ceased.

On 6 June 1930 Flight Cadet Lieutenant D. R. C Hodson RN was piloting a IIIF over Chichester, Sussex, with Corporal T. W. F. Bryan and AC1 J. E. Anning, both of the RAF, as his passengers. Anning said that they had taken off from Gosport, Hampshire, at 9 a.m. and had been flying locally for about an hour. They had just passed Tangmere Aerodrome on their left and were at 4,000 feet when the machine suddenly 'vibrated badly all over' and they heard 'a loud grinding noise'. The propeller shaft sheared, and Anning saw the propeller fly back and lodge in the starboard lower wing, damaging it very badly. Hodson immediately switched off the engine, but the aircraft quickly got out of control and he shouted 'Jump!' just as the IIIF entered a right-hand spin.

On seeing the pilot freeing himself to jump, Bryan shouted 'Come on!' and 'hopped out'. He was the first to get clear, and as the aircraft was half way through the first spin Hodson and Anning jumped. Bryan's parachute opened, and 'when he got over the excitement' he was greatly relieved to see his companions floating down two or three hundred feet below him. Bryan and Hodson made good landings, but the wind took Anning's parachute just before he alighted and he hit sideways, taking all the shock on his right leg. Fortunately, he was not seriously injured.

Group Captain Peter Heath encountered the IIIF on an FAA conversion course at Leuchars in 1931, where deck-landing technique was taught in endless hours of Aerodrome Dummy Deck Landing practice. He recalled:

> Two markers were placed on the aerodrome 70ft apart (the width of a carrier's deck). The approach was made with lots of engine but, by cocking the nose heavenwards, the forward speed was kept to a minimum (about 60kt if I remember right) and then you thumped down between the markers in as short a space as possible.
>
> Not much to it really, provided you watched for the one booby trap, which was that one or two of the aircraft had got their airspeed indicators calibrated not in knots, but in mph. Sixty knots is about 70 mph, which was fine, but if you came staggering in with the needle wavering around the 60 without realising it meant mph and not knots, you could achieve a pretty startling arrival—if you ever arrived at all. As soon as you closed the throttle, you stopped flying.

On 17 February 1932 Flying Officer G. F. Whistondale, with 450 Flight FAA on *Courageous*, became the first person to save his life using Irvin's quick-release harness. He jumped out just before his aircraft, Fairey IIIF Mk IIIB S1491, crashed into the sea and sank off Marsa Scirocco in the Mediterranean (accounts vary as to whether the carrier was at Gibraltar or Malta at the time.) Having baled out safely from his stricken machine, he alighted in the sea and had the good luck to be picked up by a small fishing boat after only twenty minutes. Whistondale expressed mild surprise at the 'complete lack of any sensation at all other than he existed after the experience', from the time he left his aircraft until his feet touched the water. He said it was quite easy to see the water coming up towards him, and he pressed the quick-release button of his harness the moment his feet touched, the parachute and harness ending up some thirty yards away. Sadly his passenger, Able Seaman J. Starley, drowned.

Tommy Lucke, who flew the IIIF on No 207 Squadron, wrote that the IIIF's handling characteristics were 'perfectly straightforward, and the aircraft had no outstanding vices'. He recalled that, although it had Handley Page slots, these were locked shut during his time with the Squadron. 'Taxying, take-off and landing required care,' he added, 'as the machines were not fitted with wheel brakes, and forward visibility was restricted by what seemed to us at the time to be a very long

nose housing the Lion XI engine.' However, they preferred their Lion-engined IIIFs to the 12mph-faster air-cooled Panther-engined Fairey Gordons of No 35 Squadron because the water-cooled Lions gave them warmer cockpits. Moreover, Lucke says, 'we were full of confidence in the reliability of the Lion engine, and in two years I never had occasion to make a forced landing because of it.'

Although none of No 207 Squadron's aircraft had blind-flying instruments, an electronically recording bank indicator was fitted to his flight commander's machine for trial purposes. Red or green lights were supposed to show when the port or starboard wing was low, and when no bank was indicated it was theoretically possible to maintain a straight course by keeping central an air bubble in a curved tube of liquid on the instrument panel. It 'was considered quite an achievement' when a flight was led in tight formation on a southerly course from cloud base at 2,000 feet until it emerged successfully at 14,000 feet, though it was 'sheer good fortune that the trial was carried out flying due south, on which heading the compass acts as an over-sensitive turn indicator'. Later flights ran into trouble owing to lack of knowledge concerning acceleration error and northerly turning error. Consequently it was concluded that the device was not suitable for safe blind flying.

On another occasion the Squadron was required to test electrically heated flying clothing during an endurance flight at 17,000 feet while carrying a full warload comprising 500 pounds of dummy bombs, plus one Vickers and one Lewis gun, both with ammunition. The heated clothing consisted of flying boots, waistcoat and gauntlets embedded with filaments attached to leads that were plugged into the pilot's cockpit instrument panels. Adjacent to the sockets were three two-position switches marked 'Full on' and 'Off'. There was no intermediate control. The aircraft took off early for the flight, which was expected to last three and a half hours, and upon reaching 10,000 feet and receiving the signal from the Flight Commander they turned on their oxygen and the three heater switches. Lucke recalls:

As we continued the climb and various parts of our anatomy became too warm, we periodically switched off the appropriate control switch until such time as we needed warming up again. About this time we became aware that the leadership of our formation, hitherto faultless, had become somewhat erratic. Without

Above: Another group of No 207 Squadron IIIFs. When Tommy Lucke flew IIIFs in this unit they had Handley Page slots fitted but they were locked shut, perhaps as a result of the adverse effect they had on stalling and spinning. Legible serials here are (Mk Is) S1178, S1205, S1202 and S1184, and (Mk IV) J91??.

warning, our leader would yaw first one way and then the other, and we had to do a lot of throttle work to stay with him. This behaviour was most unlike him as he was noted for being a most considerate leader in formation.

On landing, our flight commander stopped his engine as soon as his machine came to rest in the middle of the aerodrome and then beckoned to two of us for help. On reaching him we found that he had discarded his flying boots and was sitting in his socks, unable to bear any weight on his feet. A faulty control switch had prevented him turning off the heat for his flying boots throughout the whole flight. He played no tennis that afternoon.

Another Service pilot was John Nesbitt-Dufort, who first flew a IIIF at Leuchars and wrote in his book *Open Cockpit* (London: Speed and Sport Publications Ltd, 1970) that he 'found it to be a real old gentleman's aeroplane; rock steady, no vices and oh so easy to fly'. He said that the Lion was 'relatively trustworthy', although he had known one to shed a propeller complete with reduction gear'. He found the 'booted' version 'quite a lot of fun' when he flew it in the FAA on a floatplane course at Calshot in 1933. He had some seven hours on the landplane, and found that there was

. . . little or no difference in the handling of the two except that the seaplane may have been a shade heavier, but it was during taxying, take-off and landings that the techniques were so different. During taxying it must be remembered that while the engine was running one was always under way, i.e. one could not stop unless it was switched off. As the seaplane was not left at moorings at the end of the day it was dragged up a slipway, and this entailed beaching, which was always an exciting manoeuvre.

With an offshore wind an approach could be made head-on, switching off the engine at exactly the right distance from the shore with just enough way on to carry one to within reach of the ground crews who had waded out with trolleys to slip under the floats. This enabled the 'plane to be winched up the slipway on to the tarmac. But with an onshore wind it was a different kettle of fish. Then the drill was to approach in a wide sweep, swinging the nose out to sea at the last moment and then switching off, the aircraft would then be drifted backwards by the wind (one hoped) into the waiting hands of the ground crew. If the onshore wind was fairly strong you could pull up allstanding with the engine ticking over,

Below: Another take-off study, this time featuring IIIF Mk IIIB S1491/'53' of 450 Flight as it makes its departure from HMS *Courageous*.

Above: Fairey IIIF '81' of 824 Squadron lands on board HMS *Eagle*. There was no form of arrester gear in use at this time (other than human restraint).

then by cutting one of the mags the resultant rev drop would allow the 'plane to be blown backwards, and by switching the mag on again the drift was stopped in what should be the correct position for the ground crew.

Beaching, as can be seen, required quite a modicum of skill and with an offshore wind premature switching off of the engine could result in one being blown out to sea again feeling absolutely helpless with a dead 'stick'. Therefore one had to know quite a bit about seamanship as well as flying. Taxying with water-rudders engaged was actually fairly simple if one just realised that the speed down wind tended to be twice as fast as when taxying into wind with no brakes to slow one up, and the Solent even in those days was a very busy shipping lane.

Take-off could be quite hard work. The procedure was as follows: first, find a clear run of at least a mile and, having turned into wind, carry out the cockpit check, which included winding on a few degrees of camber, disengage water rudders and open up fully (the ordinary rudder was then pretty effective and the aircraft could easily be kept straight). The IIIF now ploughed along fussily in a cloud of spray at about 30 knots and would continue to do so indefinitely if no further action were taken, so the control column was pumped backwards and forward and this movement continued with decreasing violence until the rocking motion of the aircraft was sufficient to get the floats up on their 'steps'; when this occurred the controls were centralised. After a further quarter mile or so a gentle backward pressure on the stick resulted in one feeling a pronounced acceleration as she 'unstuck'.

When the sea was glassy and there was little or no wind with anything like a load up, one could run for miles madly rocking the IIIF fore and aft without its making any attempt to get up on its 'step'. But the wily pilot will not accept this refusal, and like putting a stubborn horse at a jump, executes a wide turn on the water and then takes off across his own wash, the roughness of which is just sufficient to allow him to hop on the 'step'. Although man-made waves can help a take-off they should be treated with caution as I seem to remember on one occasion being prematurely tossed into the air by the bow wave of the German liner *Bremen* quite a while after it had passed.

Landing was simplicity itself, assuming of course the sea was not glassy calm, as this made it difficult to judge height. The seaplane landed in the flying attitude . . . so a powered approach was made, easing off the throttle gently at about 3 feet resulting in a very slow sink on to the water. I thought the landing on water was a marvellous sensation until one was almost stopped and then for no apparent reason the IIIF would do a little curtsey. The first time it happens you feel as though she has dug the nose of her floats in and she is going over on her back, but it is only the sudden slowing up due to her coming off the 'step' again and you soon get used to the feeling. Landings could also be made in quite heavy swells, but always parallel to and never across them.

During the summer, having made sure there was a starting handle in its stowage, certain young officers used to fly round to the eastern side of the Isle of Wight and having landed, switch off and sling out a sea anchor. They would then wriggle out of their overalls and go for a swim; of course there had to be at least two on board for starting up, one at the throttles and switches and the other to crank while perched precariously on the port float.

Air Commodore Stan Quill, who flew the IIIF in the Royal New Zealand Air Force, recalled that 'Flying the IIIF has been referred to as a "gentlemanly pursuit"', and said that the aircraft was 'Steady, really steady . . . you sat a little behind the wings and they gave you this feeling that they spread out forever. Struts, wires everywhere, motor away up the front ticking away not making much noise. All controls were quite powerful at normal speeds—and one didn't really get much away from "normal" speeds in those days.'

Quill gained his initial experience by 'back seat familiarisation'. 'The Fairey IIIF [as supplied to New Zealand] had no dual controls,' he recalled, 'and so the only way to learn anything about its flying characteristics was either to jump in the front and fly it—or to jump in the back while somebody else flew it. . . . to stand in the back facing the buffeting of a 100mph-plus slipstream and at the same time try to take in all the subtle actions of a skilled pilot was really hardly on. But back seat familiarisation was a sort of ritual—you had to go through this—not unpleasant—initiation before being allowed to taste the joys of flying this rather handsome old aeroplane . . .' 'We had two such sessions,' he adds, 'one of 30 minutes and one of 50 minutes. Apart from the noise, streaming eyes and slight deafening I don't recall gaining anything.'

Referring to the variable camber, Quill wrote:

The whole of [the] trailing edge, ailerons and all, could be wound down by a wheel in the cockpit . . . at all normal weights this variable camber was not *needed* for take-off or landing. (Long since I read where −2° 'flap' was best for top speed, +4° for take-off and +8° for landing. I suspect that that must have been for floatplane operation or for full war load flying which we never used.)

What I did discover, though, was that if one throttled back, wound down full camber and reduced speed to about 5 or so m.p.h. above stalling speed . . . the old beast would just sink gently towards the ground, quite steeply: then at about 100ft, one just built up the speed a little by depressing the nose—then round out, sink gently on to the ground and run but a few feet. It was a marvellous thing to do and a comforting technique for a forced landing . . . I liked the IIIF—it had style.

At sea, however, the flaps came into their own, as Group Captain Peter Heath recalled:

. . . the aircraft had no brakes and there were no arrester wires. But the IIIF . . . did have enormous flaps. The whole trailing edge of all four wings hinged down to give a real 'clutching hand' wing section which produced perfectly safe flying conditions at 60kt (but not 60 m.p.h.). Under these conditions, arrester wires were unnecessary. I do not think . . . anyone had ever been known to go over the front end and, in fact, with a wind speed of 30kt always maintained down the deck, it really took quite a long time to catch the ship up. The only arrester system we had was that, as soon as you touched, a lot of sailors leapt out from the nets and grabbed you before you could be blown back over the 'round-down' at the stern.

Peter Heath then did a week-long IIIF seaplane conversion course at Calshot, amassing a mere 1 hour 50 minutes before being let loose, and then 6½ hours

solo to qualify on floats. It was some months later that he tried to take off in a IIIF seaplane at Gibraltar to join part of a formation send-off for *Courageous* as the carrier sailed for Malta:

> I had the pleasure of taking off first with a fully laden aircraft on a glassy sea with no wind. Remembering what I could of my whole week's experience at Calshot, I reckoned the mile and a half of harbour provided plenty of space and opened up. Nothing much happened except that clouds of spray shot up and a horrible jolting shook the craft, so the throttle was smartly shut again. I repeated the process with the stick in various parts of the cockpit but without success, so I just floated about watching the others. They did no better. In fact, we spent most of the morning thrashing round the harbour in clouds of spray, looking like wounded dabchicks, making ugly darts at passing picket boats and completely failing to get airborne.

A friendly pilot of a IIIF seaplane on a catapult cruiser provided enlightenment, and after lunch all of the pilots managed to get off and catch up with the carrier. Peter Heath explained:

> At rest a seaplane sits more or less in a flying attitude but, as you open up the engine, the shape of the floats is such that the front end is forced up and the aircraft's tail nearly goes into the water. This feels alarming and the natural reaction is to push the stick forwards to bring the tail up, which is where we went wrong. This does two things: the elevators are pushed down and immediately get the full force of large quantities of spray against them, slowing the aircraft down. Also you are thrusting the nose down and so the toes of the floats go deeper into the water, slowing you down even more. The correct drill is to keep everything central and, after a short time, the tail comes up of its own accord, the aircraft gets up on to the step and you are away. But we had forgotten that.

The IIIF's very low approach speed for deck landings of 44 knots made its landing-on characteristics almost viceless. When carriers such as *Courageous* or

Above: The view from the rear cockpit of one of a formation of IIIFs as they approach their carrier, HMS *Eagle*, for a fly-by. The ship's after lift is down, and the forward windbreak is raised.

Glorious were steaming into a fifteen-knot wind, the IIIF pilots found that some effort was required to catch them up, so a landing without arrester gear was not as perilous as might be imagined.

A first-hand account of a truly alarming experience during a catapult launch has been provided by none other than jet-engine pioneer Sir Frank Whittle. Whittle was an excellent pilot, and towards the end of 1930 he was posted to the MAEE at Felixstowe as a floatplane test pilot. His main task was catapult test work, to which he was assigned shortly after his arrival at the MAEE, and late in February 1931 he made three practice launches at RAE Farnborough. In his book *Jet* (London: Frederick Muller Ltd, 1953) he recalls:

> The length of the [catapult's] stroke was about 50 feet and in this distance the aircraft accelerated to just under 60 mph. This meant a maximum acceleration of about 2½g . . . , so that immediately before the launch it was necessary to have one's head back against the headrest provided. At first the sensation produced by this tremendous acceleration was very odd, but I found that one very soon got used to it.

For his subsequent catapult work Whittle used to go aboard HMS *Ark Royal*, a 10,000-ton tramp steamer that had been converted to a seaplane tender and had recently been fitted with an experimental catapult mounted on its forecastle deck (the ship was renamed *Pegasus* in December 1934 when the name *Ark Royal* was transferred to a new aircraft carrier), to carry out trials in the Solent. On 4 July 1932, during his fifth and last series of trials, and on the last launch of a series to test the effect of reduced wind speed along the catapult, he was carrying Flight Lieutenant F. Kirk as a passenger in IIIF Mk IIIB S1800.

Because the component of wind along the catapult was nil, the aircraft was launched at about three knots below its minimum flying speed, and the instant it left the catapult its nose rose sharply. Instantly, Whittle instinctively pushed the control column fully forward, and after the aircraft had staggered a few hundred yards in a virtually stalled attitude he was relieved to realise that it was not going to plunge into the sea. However, he did not know why the IIIF was virtually out of control, initially wondering whether the tailplane had been damaged at launch, possibly by hitting a steam hoist that had not been swung clear. When he glanced over his shoulder, however, he saw a body lying face down on the tailplane, and assumed that he had somehow 'collected' an airman who had been working on the catapult.

Gathering his unsettled nerves, he looked again, and this time realised that the person on the tailplane was Kirk, who had now contrived to adopt a sitting position with his back against one of the bracing wires to the fin. Kirk gave Whittle a thumbs-up with his left hand and mimed 'Okay'. 'Had I been in a better position to appreciate it,' wrote Whittle, 'I might have been very amused at what was really a rather funny sight, because Kirk was wearing a borrowed flying helmet which was much too large for him and when he opened his mouth the wind distended his cheeks in a most grotesque manner. He seemed far less alarmed than I felt.'

The aircraft was at about 60 feet, but Whittle found that it would not be easy to descend because, when he throttled back, the tail dropped owing to the reduced slipstream. He therefore had to keep the throttle open, and because Kirk was completely blanking off the rudder he was unable to turn into wind. Luckily there was only a light wind, and he had just enough control to enable him to force the nose down very slightly, and he gradually lost height. To complicate matters, a German liner was crossing his path, and he needed to get the IIIF on the water before he flew into its side. He managed this with some 200 yards to spare, alighting by easing the throttle back slowly with the stick fully forward.

Opposite: A dramatic head-on overhead view of HMS *Furious* with a IIIF being pushed back off the front lift and the windbreak raised. Note also the palisades along the deck edges, to prevent errant aircraft from going over the side.

When S1800's floats touched the water after its frightening five-minute flight, Whittle still had half throttle, and the captain of the liner generously turned to port to allow him more sea room.

In the process of clambering along the rear fuselage to return to his rear cockpit, Kirk nearly put his feet through the structure, inflicting the only damage sustained by the aircraft throughout the incident. Whittle was 'almost in a state of nervous collapse', but Kirk appeared 'quite calm and collected'. Weak and trembling, Whittle looked at him and said, 'My God!', to which Kirk replied, 'What are you worrying about?'. 'After we were hoisted aboard,' Whittle recalled, 'pink gins were pressed upon us from all directions by a number of very relieved naval officers.'

The event was filmed, so it was possible to see what had happened. Kirk's gloves were slippery with the glycerine used as a lubricant for the catapult, and he had lost his grip on the front rim of his cockpit. Shooting back to the rear of the long cockpit, he had bounced into the air, turning as he went. Such had been his presence of mind that he had grabbed the fin bracing wire with one hand before any part of him had touched the tailplane.

Any damage to S1800 must have been superficial, as Whittle carried out another six launches in it on the following day, and five more the day after that.

Another pilot's vivid impressions of the IIIF seaplane were provided by Wing Commander S. J. 'Beau' Carr in his delightful auto-biography *You are not Sparrows* (London: Ian Allan, 1975), recounting his interwar flying experiences in the RAF. Having been flying Westland Wapitis with No 55 Squadron in Iraq, Carr was posted to Calshot in 1931 to undergo a conversion course on to seaplanes. He had never flown a IIIF landplane, though he was familiar with it, so only encountered it in its 'booted' form. He remarked that '… the IIIF claimed affection of a sort from most of those who flew it,' and recalled:

> In the cockpit you had the feeling of sitting in the middle of a very large machine. Its performance was far from electrifying: it cruised at 100mph, reached a maximum of 120, and stalled at around 50.
>
> The greybeards at Calshot were full of awful warnings about the inadvisability of attempting even the mildest aerobatics. They said especially that it must not be side-slipped or spun because of the enormous keel surface of the floats plus the long fuselage.
>
> All of which turned out to be incorrect. You could loop, spin, stall-turn and side-slip the thing like any other aeroplane. Although it spun fast it recovered quickly, but you needed at least 1,500 feet in which to effect recovery to level flight from where you stopped the spin.

At the end of his four-week course Carr was posted to the School of Naval Co-operation at Lee-on-Solent, just across the water, where FAA officers were trained as observers and naval ratings as telegraphist air gunners. Here he continued flying the IIIF sea-plane:

> Once in the air a twin-float seaplane handles like any other aeroplane and the only thing one needed

to learn all over again was the take-off and landing, during both of which the fore and aft movements of the stick were almost exactly the reverse of landplane technique. Instead of shoving the stick forward to get the tail up, you held it hard back to begin with, to get the toes of the floats clear of the water. You pushed the stick forward to get her up on the step—that is, in the hydroplaning attitude—and then, as flying speed was reached, eased gently back and she would come off nicely. A choppy sea was the ideal water condition, since it allowed air to get under the step. It took a long run to unstick in a flat calm.

Landing presented no problem; you put the aircraft on to the water in a slightly tail-down attitude and as the speed dropped off you hauled the stick hard back into your guts. Again, this was to hold the toe of the floats well up, otherwise, especially in a rough sea, they could dig in and the whole outfit could turn over on its back.

As speed was lost she would gently adopt a naturally horizontal floating attitude, but landing on a flat glassy calm was a hazard because of the difficulty of judging height. This problem was accentuated in clear shallow water because in such conditions you could often see the bottom, which might be twenty or thirty feet down, but could seldom gauge the actual surface, and the danger here was of flying straight into the drink without holding off.

To overcome this difficulty, it was usual to have a line of buoys, strung out like a flare path, by which to judge height. Alternatively, since a flat calm denoted no wind, you could land parallel and close into the shore, looking at the beach instead of the water.

Below: Deck handlers manœuvre a Fairey IIIF of 824 Squadron on board *Eagle* in April 1933, watched by a healthy number of spectators. The carrier was recommissioned on 28 March that year following a major refit at Devonport, and on Saturday 29 April she left Portsmouth bound for the China Station, there to relieve HMS *Hermes*.

Unlike flying boats, which stayed out at moorings all the time, a float plane, being more vulnerable to rough seas and high winds, had to be brought up the slipway and into the hangars. For this beaching a trolley was fixed to the floats and a winch cable hooked on to it to haul the aircraft up the slipway. This was the job of the waders; airmen and sailors who spent most of the day up to their armpits in water. All right in the summer but not very jolly in winter. They got a daily rum ration but could opt for 2d. a day in lieu if they were teetotal.

It called for careful judgement of taxying speed, wind, tide and drift in order to choose the right moment to switch off as you approached the slip. If you cut the engine too soon, especially with an offshore wind, the waders would be out of their depth before they could reach the aircraft with the winch wire and the trolley; and there you would be, alone in your idiotic predicament and drifting out of control back to sea, for there was no other way of restarting the engine than by the standard method of two men, one each side of the engine nacelle, winding away with the starting handles.

If you left it too late before cutting the switches you would clout the concrete slipway, to the detriment of the floats, and be in grave danger of decapitating one of the waders with that great big spinning metal prop.

One extraordinary 'slipway landing' at Lee-on-Solent is graphically described by Carr:

Twice a year a bunch of Admirals and Post Captains arrived from the Senior Officers' tactical course at Portsmouth for air experience. Few of them had ever flown and they didn't know what it was all about. No doubt they were destined to command aircraft carriers.

Bill King, who weighed seventeen stone and drank a bottle of whisky a day (he retired from rugby football at nineteen), was not the best of pilots; his flying somewhat lacked finesse. He drew an admiral as a passenger.

There was an offshore wind and on returning to base Bill decided to do a slipway landing. We all liked doing this. There were not many ways in which you could be a split-arse with a seaplane, but this was one of them. The idea was to approach straight towards the slipway and touch down at a point which would enable you to complete the landing run with engine switched off just short of the slip, so that the aircraft would very gently touch bottom and be grabbed by the waders.

It called for good judgement and precise attention to approach speed, strength of wind and condition of sea.

Below: A Fairey IIIF Mk IIIB on charge to the School of Naval Co-operation and seen here occupying the slipway at Lee-on-Solent in 1934, S1523/ 'B', suffered an undercarriage collapse while alighting on 17 April 1935 and sank. It was struck off charge as damaged beyond repair on 3 May that year.

Bill came in at a good 100mph, touched down about fifty yards from shore, still going like a bat out of hell, bounced straight out of the water, shot up the slipway with sparks flying from the floats, crossed the road and shuddered to a standstill on the parade ground right in front of the hangars.

The Admiral climbed out beaming, patted Bill on the shoulder, thanked him warmly and trundled away to the white-faced reception party, firmly convinced that this was how seaplanes were always landed. Nobody disillusioned him.

Above: Another of the SoNC's charges at Lee-on-Solent was Mk IIIB S1825/'D'. After being struck off charge as damaged beyond repair on 18 May 1936, it was at RAE Farnborough by 15 September that year.

Policing the Empire

The Fairey IIIF in Royal Air Force Overseas Service

IF one looks at the key contribution of the ubiquitous two- or three-seat biplane class in the RAF of the interwar years, it soon becomes clear that three families of aeroplane design were paramount—the classic Hart variants from Hawker, the Wapiti/Wallace from Westland and Fairey's IIIF/Gordon/Seal series. In terms of manufacturing output, the IIIF series took second place, the respective figures totalling around 2,600 for the Hart range (including the Ospreys for the FAA), over 800 from the Fairey factory (again including the seagoing varieties) and more than 600 aeroplanes from the Wapiti/Wallace stable. They all shared a common characteristic in their ability to operate reliably in rugged conditions of terrain, especially overseas, where what used to be known as 'policing the Empire' was the cardinal *raison d'être* of the RAF in its early days of independence.

Below: The 1927 Cape Flight IIIF S1143/'3' runs up its Lion at Heliopolis, ready to depart.

As the chosen types to supersede the obsolete D.H.9A and Bristol Fighter of 1918 vintage which had served so valiantly in the 1920s, the Fairey IIIF and Wapiti were initially rival contenders. In the event, though, they became contemporaries because each type exhibited characteristics suitable for a particular geographical zone. The Wapiti, dominant in Iraq and the North-West Frontier of India, lacked the facility to operate equally well both as a landplane and seaplane so decisively exhibited by the IIIF, which found its ideal habitat in such territories

Above: Pre-production Fairey IIIF 'Interim Type' S1139 was the first of ten converted from IIIDs on the production line. Delivered to the FAA at Gosport and passed to the RAF, by December 1926 it had been shipped to India, and is seen here as '2' with No 60 Squadron at Lahore in India for theatre trials. It was short-lived; on 12 March 1927 S1139 was burnt out at Peshawar and written off, Flying Officer R. O. Rigg, LAC P. J. Sexton and LAC W. J. Meaden all being killed.

Left: Another of the ten pre-production 'Interim Types', S1141 is here seen at No 4 Flying Training School, Abu Sueir, Egypt. It had been aircraft No 4 for the 1927 flight from Heliopolis to the Cape and back. After being rebuilt as SR1141 it served with Nos 45 and 47 Squadrons.

Left: This photograph of 'Interim Type' S1145 bears, on the reverse, the inscription 'Fairey IIIF from Aircraft Depot Middle East. With AVM Webb Bowen & pilot Wing Cmdr Stent [?] arrived 84 [Squadron? Based at Shaibah, Iraq] 3rd Oct 1927. Left next day.' After being rebuilt as SR1145, it served with No 47 Squadron.

Left: Flight Lieutenant S. D. Macdonald of No 47 Squadron tests Fairey IIIF Mk I S1141 for the 1927 Cairo–Cape Flight at No 4 Flying Training School, Abu Sueir.

as Egypt, the Sudan and Transjordan. For reasons which are less evident, in view of the brilliant performance of the same manufacturer's Fox, the IIIF was also selected to equip three day bomber squadrons in the United Kingdom.

As previously explained, the IIIF was a linear descendant of the Fairey IIIA, IIIB and IIIC seaplanes which had originated in World War I, the IIIC seeing action with the RAF in North Russia in 1919. This line culminated in the IIID, available both as a landplane and seaplane, and indeed, as described in the opening chapter of this book, the first IIIFs were converted on the IIID production line.

The IIIF's nautical origins are reflected in the fact that the Fleet Air Arm used it in considerably larger numbers than the RAF itself, although the RAF was in fact the first to take it into squadron service, with No 47 at Khartoum in the Sudan in December 1927. The six IIIF Mk Is concerned, S1141–S1146, had been diverted from the original batch often originally intended as three-seat spotter-reconnaissance aeroplanes for the FAA and adapted instead as two-seat general-purpose aircraft. This basic difference remained throughout the IIIF's long career with the RAF and the FAA.

In command at Khartoum when the first IIIFs arrived was Air Commodore Charles Rumney Samson, Chief Staff Officer, Middle East, the celebrated RNAS pilot who in 1927 had been involved in pioneering long-distance formation training flights across Africa by the RAF. Such exercises in 'showing the flag' became a familiar feature of IIIF activities, and No 47 Squadron completed return flights from Cairo to Cape Town in 1927, 1928 and 1929. The 11,000-mile 1927 flight, made by four Mk Is, S1141–S1144, led by Samson, left Heliopolis, Cairo, on 30 March 1927, reached Cape Town on 21 April and arrived back at Heliopolis on 22 May. Samson's fellow pilots were Squadron Leader R. S. Maxwell, Flight Lieutenant S. D. Macdonald, and Flying Officer D. L. G. Brett. Accompanying Samson in the lead aircraft was Flight Lieutenant D. J. Blackford, acting as navigator; sergeant engineers were carried in the other three aircraft. Although they were flying in an aircraft type new to the Service, the flight, carried out in accordance with a prearranged schedule, was virtually trouble-free. During the flight the aircraft took part in a variety of inter-Service events and engagements. From Nairobi southwards they were accompanied by South African Air Force Airco D.H.9s. The two remaining Mk Is went to India, one of them, S1139, ending its life in a crash there.

No 47 later became the first squadron to receive the RAF general-purpose version of the IIIF in its initial production form, the Mk IVC, some of the first twenty-five (J9053–J9077) being shipped out to Khartoum. The 1928 flight, using four Mk IVCs, was led by Flight Lieutenant O. Gayford, who later entered RAF history books as the pilot of Fairey Long Range Monoplane K1991, which captured the world distance record for Great Britain (5,309 miles from Cranwell to Walvis Bay, South Africa) in February 1933. Unfortunately, while heading south after leaving Cairo on 1 March 1928, Gayford, carrying the AOC Middle East, Air Vice-Marshal Webb-Bowen, crashed on take-off from Ndola, Northern Rhodesia. The aircraft's occupants escaped injury. The four-aircraft 1929 flight that departed from Cairo on 12 February fared less well. During the return flight the IIIF flown by Flying Officer Y. W. Burnett crashed at Gwelo, Southern Rhodesia, killing the passenger sergeant fitter and injuring Burnett.

As one of the RAF's few amphibious units, No 47 Squadron also converted several of its IIIFs into seaplanes for operations from the Nile at Khartoum. Tasks undertaken included surveying the upper reaches of the Nile and conducting anti-piracy patrols along the Red Sea, sometimes alighting with a boarding officer near suspect vessels.

Several long-range flights were also undertaken by No 14 Squadron, based at Amman in Transjordan at that time. In 1929 four IIIFs of this unit, led by Squadron Leader F. J. Vincent, flew from Aboukir, Egypt, to Nigeria and back, and Squadron Leader E. L. Howard-Williams led a similar flight in 1930. This squadron also made the 1930 Cairo-Cape return flight, and Wing Commander A. T. Harris (later 'Bomber Harris'), flying his personal aircraft, led a return flight by three IIIFs from Heliopolis to East Africa.

Another Middle East IIIF squadron which participated in the long-range flights was No 8, which completed an Aden–Cairo return trip, led by Squadron Leader R. S. Sorley, in 1932. These IIIF flights must be seen as quite remarkable

Below: The 'Interim Type' IIIFs of No 47 Squadron used for the 1927 Cape Flight on Heliopolis Aerodrome. The only serial visible is S1146, 'Black 1', second from right.

AUTHOR'S COLLECTION

achievements, considering the difficulties of operating without any modern navigational aids over largely uncharted territory.

On the operational side, the IIIF squadrons gave a good account of themselves in action against dissident tribesmen, of which there were many in the mandated territories. The Aden Protectorate (arguably the most unpopular posting in the RAF owing to its climate) saw No 8 Squadron's IIIFs in residence at Khormaksar for over seven years, the longest service period of any IIIF unit. It was wholly responsible for the security of the protectorate from 1928, and did not relinquish its IIIFs for Vickers Vincents until March 1935. The Squadron began replacing its D.H.9As with IIIFs in 1928. Though the new mounts offered only slight improvements in speed, range and bomb load, they were more comfortable. The Squadron was in action against the marauding Suhebis tribe from January to March 1929. This large tribe had caused no trouble while it was receiving payments to encourage good behaviour, but when the payments ceased it raided the Lahej district, destroying property and stealing cattle. Having issued advance warnings, from 30 January to 5 March No 8 Squadron used mainly small incendiaries to destroy crops and dwellings, which resulted in peace being restored. By 27 March terms had been agreed by the tribal chiefs, who paid compensation fines.

The primary task of British ground and flying forces in Aden in the early 1930s was to improve communications between the numerous villages and tribal towns. This included building roads and establishing dozens of temporary landing grounds. As well as providing air support for this work, No 8 Squadron was frequently required to perform 'demonstration flights' and drop leaflets over potential troublespots, thus bringing the offenders to heel and pre-empting the need for operations of a more violent nature. Actual bombing sorties were rare, and prior warning was always given in order to minimise human casualties. In addition, the unit carried out fortnightly mail deliveries between bases and transported political officers and officials to outlying towns and villages.

During the Cyprus riots of 1931 a detachment of IIIFs flew to the island from Egypt. Over the Mediterranean they were met by the seaplane IIIF from HMS *London*, which took over as navigational leader. The IIIFs of No 14 Squadron, based at Amman in Transjordan, co-operated with ground forces (including RAF armoured cars and the Trans-Jordan Frontier Force) during troubles in Palestine in 1929–32, firing their guns on several occasions to disperse recalcitrant tribes.

Left: Fairey IIIF Mk I S1190, c/n F914, was aircraft No 1 of the 1928 Cape Town to Cairo Flight, and later joined No 47 Squadron.

Helwan-based No 45 Squadron, which had re-formed at Heliopolis in April 1927 with D.H.9As, operated IIIFs from August 1929 to December 1935, carrying out patrol duties in Egypt and Palestine. It had detachments at Amman, Gaza, Ismailia, Hinaidi, Mosul, Shaibah and Eastleigh. As with other IIIF squadrons mentioned earlier, its aircraft made annual long-range training flights, flying from Egypt to West Africa and back in 1929 and 1931.

No 47 Squadron at Khartoum, which received IIIFs in place of its D.H.9As in April 1928, co-operated closely with the Sudan Defence Force in regular frontier patrols and took full advantage of the IIIF's capacity to operate on floats, flying its seaplanes (which were converted back to landplane configuration when required) from the River Nile.

Perhaps the most outstanding example of IIIF floatplane use, aside from that in the FAA, of course, was that of No 202 Squadron, based at Calafrana in Malta, which had as its prime task co-operation with the Mediterranean Fleet from July 1930. Rather oddly, during its tenure of IIIF seaplanes, it was described in the official *Air Force List* as a flying-boat squadron. Over five years were to elapse before the designation was given reality by the arrival of Supermarine Scapa flying boats in August 1935.

Below: Another view of the IIIFs of No 47 Squadron used for the 1927 Cape Flight— probably the same line-up as that on page 85 though from a different angle. The identities are revealed: (left to right) S1143/'3' (c/n F884), S1146/ '1', S1144/'2' and S1141/'4'.

Above: Three IIIFs of No 8 Squadron based at Khormaksar, Aden: (front to rear) Mk IVM/A J9664/'M', Mk IVB K1711/'P' and Mk IVM/A J9671/'N'.

Left, upper: Fairey IIIF Mk IVM J9166/'C' of No 8 Squadron making a formation flight 'for Christmas cards' in September 1930.

Left: An air-to-air study of Mk IVC (GP) seaplane J9053/'M' of No 8 Squadron. This aircraft, the first production Mk IVC for the RAF, initially flew general-purpose trials at the A&AEE. It later crashed at Aden—see page 97.

AUTHOR'S COLLECTION

AUTHOR'S COLLECTION

Above: IIIF Mk IVC J9066 of
No 8 Squadron being hoisted
at Maala in March 1929. Notice
the padded hold-off pole on
the left.

Left: First flown on 28
February 1928, IIIF Mk IVC
J9070/'Y' was with No 8
Squadron at Aden from
December 1928 to March 1929.
It was converted to a seaplane
in January 1929. The non-
standard ground-handling
dollies are noteworthy.

Right: Three aircraft of 'A'
Flight No 8 Squadron in
formation. They are J9133/'A'
and J9134/'B'—both Mk IVC/
Ms with metal fuselages and
wooden wings—and J9076/'D',
a Mk IVC. J9134 crashed at
Khormaksar on 26 July 1930.

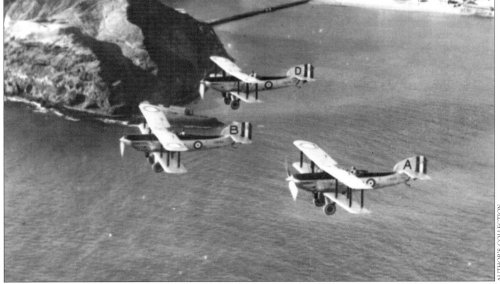

AUTHOR'S COLLECTION

Above: Another No 8 Squadron IIIF Mk IVC–J9055/'P' of 'B' Flight, in pristine condition. Conspicuous are the Scarff gun ring on the rear cockpit and the absence of Handley Page slots on the upper-wing leading edge at this stage.
Below: Mk IVC J9066 of 'B' Flight No 8 Squadron under tow in March 1929. The Squadron's 'winged 8' badge is carried on the fin.
Right: This photograph of 'Smith and James' in front of a No 8 Squadron IIIF at Aden in 1929 provides a good view of the Scarff ring mounting on the rear cockpit.
Far right: A IIIF seaplane of 'C' Flight, No 8 Squadron, has its wings folded, October 1929.

Above: No 8 Squadron's IIIF Mk IVC J9055/'P' aloft in 1929, showing the extent of the undercarriage legs' stroke when they were not under compression.

Right: An No 8 Squadron IIIF Mk IVC, J9065, in an unhappy state. This aircraft later went to the Training Base at Leuchars in Scotland.

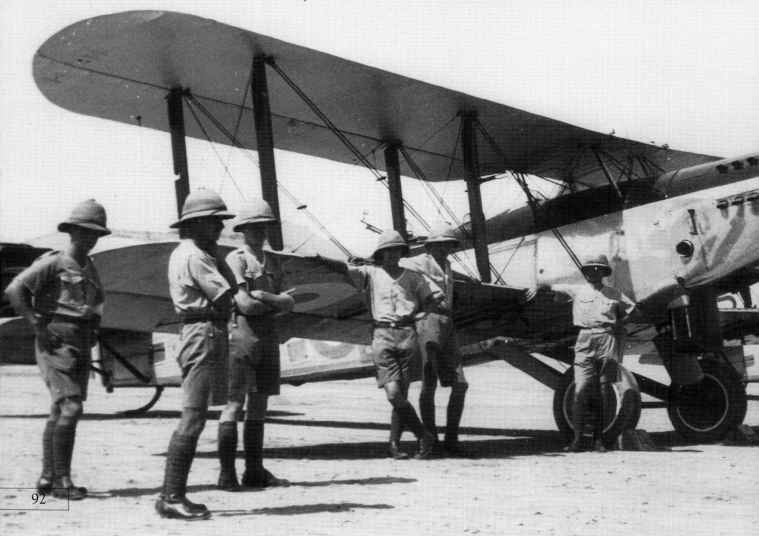

Left and below: IIIF Mk IVC (GP) of No 8 Squadron, J9073/ 'N' had Flying Officer Danbury and Flight Lieutenant Dickson on board when it ended up like this on 18 May 1929.

Below : The Fairey IIIFs of No 8 (B) Squadron lined up for the AOC's inspection in June 1929.

Right: Another view of No 8 Squadron's J9073/'N' following its inelegant landing. The aircraft went back to Fairey for reconditioning on 21 August 1931, and after a spell 'at home' with No 35 Squadron it was converted into a Gordon.

AUTHOR'S COLLECTION

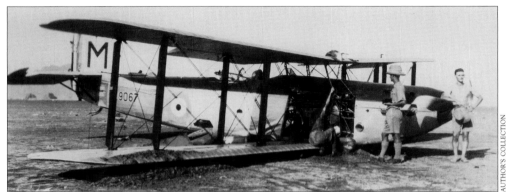

AUTHOR'S COLLECTION

Above: A No 8 Squadron IIIF Mk IVC seaplane running up its Lion engine—probably J9070, which was fitted with 'sea boots' in January 1929. Left and below: This No 8 Squadron IIIF Mk IVC, J9067/'M', had its undercarriage collapse on landing at Khormaksar and was also 'sent home', where it was converted into a Gordon and then served on No 207 Squadron.

Below: Yet another No 8 Squadron IIIF with its tail in the air, this time Mk IVC J9062/'L', which went back to its maker on 8 May 1929 and was converted into an all-metal-airframe Mk IVM, after which it served with No 207 Squadron and was subsequently converted into a Gordon.

AUTHOR'S COLLECTION

AUTHOR'S COLLECTION

AUTHOR'S COLLECTION

AUTHOR'S COLLECTION

AUTHOR'S COLLECTION

AUTHOR'S COLLECTION

Top, left and right: An un-happy end for Fairey IIIF Mk IVC (GP) J9076/'D' of 'A' Flight No 8 Squadron at Dhala. Following the crash the engine was dismantled and removed and then the airframe was burnt.

Above, left and below: Ser-geants Penwarn and Watson are named as the aircrew when this 'taxying' mishap occurred involving IIIF J9143(?)/'N' of No 8 Squadron at Aden. The snaps are dated 25 March 1930.

AUTHOR'S COLLECTION

Right: The remains of No 8
Squadron's Mk IVC J9059,
looking as though the aircraft
may well have been a victim of
the IIIF's poor spin recovery
qualities.

Left and below: Squadron
Leader Betts was in No 8
Squadron IIIF Mk IVC (GP)
J9055/'P' when it nosed over
at Aden on 28 January 1930.
Notice that aircraft's callsign is
carried inboard beneath the
lower wings.

Right: A photograph of No 8
Squadron's IIIF Mk IVC (GP)
floatplane J9053/'M' aloft—see
also page 88—formating on
another of its kind.
Below: The same machine
ashore, on beaching gear that
looks like a local product.

Right: J9053 again, having
crashed on take-off from Aden
Harbour on 30 January 1931.

Right: Seen here in Iraq, this is IIIF Mk IVM/A J9829/'M' of No 14 Squadron. It became Gordon JR9829 in 1935.

Below: Aviatrix Amy Johnson takes a close look at IIIF Mk IVM J9166/'C' of No 8 Squadron in the Middle East in May 1930, during her flight to Australia. At that time the Squadron was based at Khormaksar, Aden, some distance from Miss Johnson's route.

AUTHOR'S COLLECTION

AUTHOR'S COLLECTION

Below: Pilot Officer Henrell, Sergeant Hill (in cockpit) and Sergeant Thompson 'handing over J9055/P to ARS [Aircraft Repair Section]' at Aden in January 1930—presumably as a result of the mishap depicted in the photographs on page 96.

AUTHOR'S COLLECTION

Above: De Havilland Puss Moth G-ABKZ taxies up to a reception committee at a base somewhere in the Middle East, with RAF Fairey IIIFs close at hand; that coded 'P' in front of the Bessoneau hangar is probably S1192 or S1193, both of these Mk Is having been delivered to No 14 Squadron in the latter half of 1929. The unit was based at Ramleh and Amman from 1920 to 1939, undertaking patrol duties in Palestine and Transjordan, and Puss Moth G-ABKZ was owned by Squadron Leader Frank Soden, who was based in Amman from 1931. On an occasion in 1933 it was loaned to Lady Mountbatten, who flew it on a Middle Eastern tour, and these photographs may relate to that event.

Below: These four early IIIFs serving with No 45 Squadron all have an 'R' inserted in their serial numbers, denoting that they have been rebuilt. This was common with wooden-framed aircraft serving in the Middle East, where the heat

dried out the timber, shrinking it and causing the airframes to lose rigidity or to become distorted; it was for this very reason that the Air Ministry began specifying that its aircraft have all-metal airframes. These four are SR1144 and SR1146, both pre-production 'Interim Types', and SR1179 and SR1181, a pair of Mk Is. All were rebuilt at Aircraft Depot Middle East, Aboukir, in the late 1920s and early 1930s.

99

Right: The diagonal stripes later applied to the fins of No 45 Squadron's IIIFs are displayed here on Mk IV (GP) J9805. The stripes were red and blue, with red uppermost. The diamond in the middle of the stripe contained a pale blue image of a flying camel above the unit's motto on a scroll. The individual aircraft numbers were done away with.

Left: Fairey IIIF J9640/'4' of No 45 Squadron, one of the original batch of IIIFs taken on charge by the unit when it was based in Palestine. The first No 45 Squadron IIIF to amass 500 flying hours, it was rebuilt as JR9640, but its career came to an abrupt end when it hit a tree on approach to the Wajir Landing Ground on 4 January 1936.

Right: The two nearest Mk IVM/As in this photograph are J9657/'2' and J9659/'3' of No 45 Squadron, both of which had previously served in No 14 Squadron. The former subsequently became Gordon JR9657.

Left: A Mk IV from the same batch was J9656, seen here as '9' of 45 Squadron. It was later passed to No 47 Squadron, was then rebuilt at Aboukir and serialled JR9656, was returned to No 45 Squadron and finally was rebuilt as a Gordon and re-issued to that same unit. It was struck off charge on 6 February 1937 as beyond economical repair.

Opposite, top: The three IIIF Mk Is used for No 45 Squadron's West Africa Flight of 1929 over Cairo flying over the Nile and Gezirah Island—(front to rear) SR1171/'N2' (white fin), SR1174/'N1' (red fin) and SR1172/'N3' (blue fin).

Left: Fairey IIIF Mk I S1181/ 'N3' of No 45 Squadron under guard during its service prior to rebuilding. The two rows of exhaust stubs on the starboard side are evident here.

Below: Mk IV M/A J9642 of No 45 Squadron in basic Service finish, with no unit or individual markings; this photograph may be compared with the upper two images on page 102, which show progressive changes to the *décor*.

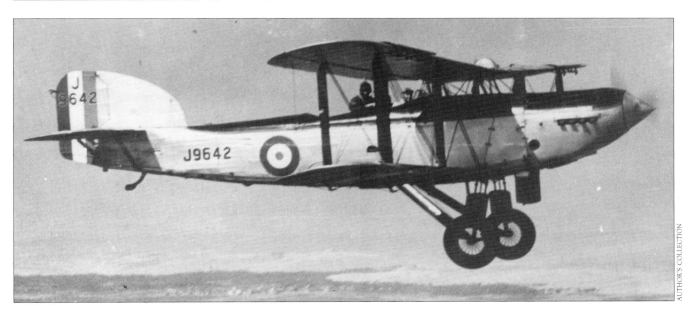

Left and below: J9642 of No 45 Squadron having now acquired the individual number '1' on its fin (left), and with the number replaced by the diagonal stripe (below). After being rebuilt and converted to a Gordon in 1934, JR9642 stalled and crashed in the sea off Aqaba, Jordan, on 3 February 1936, while serving with a detached flight of No 6 Squadron.

Below: Photographed at the time it had become the second of No 45 Squadron's aeroplanes to amass 1,000 hours of flying time, J9653 carries both its old individual number, '10', on its rear fuselage top decking, and the diagonal fin stripes. The personnel are, from left to right, Corporal Tibble, Flight Sergeant Ottoway, Sergeant White, Squadron Leader Francis Vincent and Flying Officer Arthur Combe.

Above: All twelve of No 45 Squadron's IIIFs arranged in a circle, with personnel inside forming the number '45', June 1930

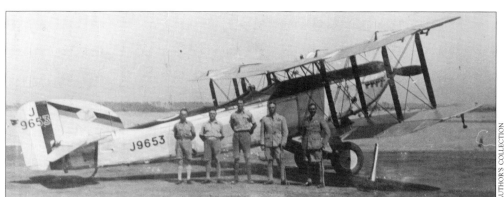

Left, upper: Led by Squadron Leader H. W. L. Sanders, IIIFs of No 45 Squadron fly over the desert near the Nile. This photograph was taken in connection with the RAF Pageant held at Heliopolis on 23 February 1934.
Below: A mass formation take-off by three flights of No 45 Squadron IIIFs, probably for a rehearsal for the 1931 RAF Middle East Display.

Below: Nine IIIFs of No 45 Squadron pass the Pyramids at Giza in line abreast—one of the most difficult formations to hold—as they rehearse for the RAF Middle East Display of 1931.

103

Left: Sergeant Tomkins aloft in Mk IV J9655/7 of 'B' Flight No 45 Squadron on 2 April 1930, flying from Cairo to Khartoum.

Below: In 1931 No 45 Squadron was again chosen to make the West Africa Flight. The four aircraft, seen here carrying their specially allotted numbers and practising over Cairo, are K1703/'1', K1704/'2', K1705/'3' and K1713/'4'.

Bottom: Mk IVs J9662 and J9653 of 'C' Flight No 45 Squadron formate for the camera and show off the IIIF's well-proportioned lines.

Left, upper: Three No 45 Squadron IIIF seaplanes over the Nile; the aircraft in the centre is J9677.

Below, left: Three IIIF Mk Is of 'A' Flight No 47 Squadron over Khartoum, with S1173 nearest. Notice the hangars and aircraft in the lower foreground. Below, right: J9653 (nearest), J9662 and J 9650 with earlier markings. This photograph clearly shows the Handley Page wing slots and the presentation of the callsigns on the upper fuselage decking.

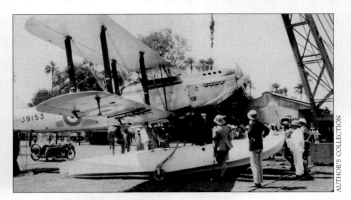

This spread: A series of photographs depicting Fairey IIIF Mk IV C/M seaplane J9153 of No 47 Squadron being lowered on to the Nile at Khartoum (left and right), taxying (background image) and in flight with S1173 for company (immediately below).

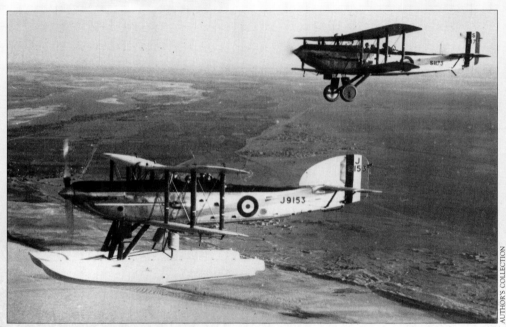

Far right: Photographed on the Nile at Khartoum on Easter Monday in March 1932, IIIF Mk IVB K1702 of No 45

Squadron has supply containers attached under its wings. A lower-fuselage access panel behind the engine has been

removed. The tail of J9806, a Mk IVM/A, is on the left. Both aircraft have landplane tailskids rather than the

handling rail often seen on IIIF seaplanes.

AUTHOR'S COLLECTION

AUTHOR'S COLLECTION

AUTHOR'S COLLECTION

Left, top: Three No 47 Squadron IIIFs in line abreast over the Blue Nile Bridge. S1173 is nearest.

Left, centre: A quartet of No 47 Squadron Fairey IIIFs at Kosti. The nearest machine is S1176, a Mk I.

Left, bottom: Mk I S1174 of No 47 Squadron at Kosti. This aircraft had participated in the 1928 Cairo–Cape Town–Cairo Flight.

Right, upper: Seaplane J9153 leads other IIIFs of No 47 Squadron alongside the Nile at Khartoum. The two nearest landplanes are Mk IVC/M J9149 and Mk I S1173.

Left, lower: Another view of No 47 Squadron's Mk I S1174 at Kosti. Below: Three rebuilt Mk Is of No 47 Squadron— SR1141, SR1193 and SR1145— at Kassala.

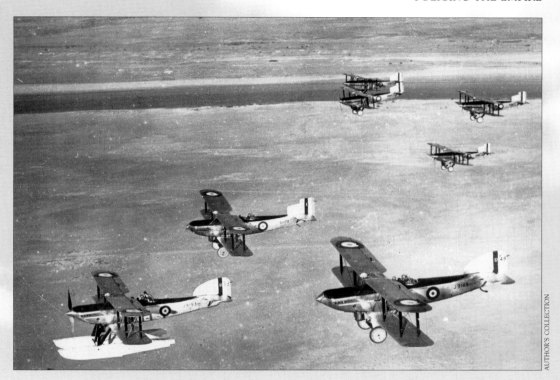

Top left: The wings of a No 47
Squadron IIIF provide much-
needed shade at El Fasher.
Left: Another No 47 Squadron
IIIF seaplane, Mk IVM J9156,
in a scenic setting at Khartoum. It appears to have
suffered some damage to its
port elevator.

Above: Another anonymous IIIF of No 47 Squadron on the shore of the Nile at Khartoum. Notice the beaching gear in the right foreground.
Left: This taxying No 47 Squadron IIIF at 'Lake No' appears to be devoid of any serial number.

Left: An anonymous No 47 Squadron IIIF seaplane attempts to hide from the photographer at Malakal.
Right: Refuelling a No 47 Squadron IIIF seaplane on Lake Yirrul. Perhaps the lady in the dugout canoe is a pilot's sweetheart about to go for a 'flip'?

AUTHOR'S COLLECTION

AUTHOR'S COLLECTION

AUTHOR'S COLLECTION

Left: A No 47 Squadron IIIF under tow on the Blue Nile. Above: Looking back over the tail of J9161 at another No 47 Squadron IIIF seaplane.

Below: Four No 47 Squadron IIIFs at El Fasher. The nearest and third aircraft are Mk IVs J9149 and J9140, respectively.

Left, upper: As well as carrying supply containers, this Mk IVM seaplane, K1159, is sporting a red fin bearing No 47 Squadron's emblem of the time—a pyramid above a crane (the ornithological variety) and squadron number and the motto 'Sans Peur'.

AUTHOR'S COLLECTION

AUTHOR'S COLLECTION

Above: Interim Type IIIF SR1144 in an unfortunate attitude at Kosti. As S1144 this aircraft had flown as Number 2 on the 1927 Cape Flight, and had been rebuilt at Aboukir before joining No 47 Squadron. Left: A *contretemps* with *terra firma*, apparently at Aboukir in 1930 or 1931, has left IIIF Mk IVM JR9156, ex No 47 Squadron, in an unhappy state. Perhaps this explains why the aircraft was converted to a Gordon shortly thereafter.

AUTHOR'S COLLECTION

Left: Ancient and 'modern' modes of transport juxtaposed on the Nile: a heavily laden dhow passes Fairey IIIF Mk IVC (GP) J9060, with its cockpit and engine protected from the sun. This aircraft was with the Basra Seaplane Flight from May 1928, with No 47 Squadron from April 1929 until January 1930 and in Palestine from March until May 1931. From February 1932 to September 1933 it served on the Communications Flight at Aboukir.

Below: Another view of J9060 on the Nile, almost certainly at the same mooring. Does 'A.B.3' on the mooring lighter relate to Aboukir?

AUTHOR'S COLLECTION

AUTHOR'S COLLECTION

AUTHOR'S COLLECTION

Left: After taking part in the 1927 Cairo–Cape Flight, 'Interim Type' IIIF S1143 remained with No 47 Squadron and was rebuilt at Aboukir, re-emerging as SR1143. It subsequently served with No 14 Squadron from August 1929, and then joined the Communications Flight at Heliopolis. It stalled on landing and crashed on 4 April 1931, killing AC1s D. Golphin and J. A. S. Thomas, 'other occupants' being seriously injured.

Top: An intimate air-to-air study of Mk IVM/A J9810 of No 47 Squadron and its topee-hatted occupants. The badge on the red fin appears to lack the motto in this instance. The slats are fully retracted against the upper wing leading edge.
Above: Captioned 'One of our recent crashes, March 1931. All three occupants badly injured': IIIF Mk IV C/M JR9151 of No 47 Squadron.
Below: This line-up of IIIF Mk IVM/As is dated 6 January 1931. A note on the back of the photograph identifies the nearest machine as J9813, 'my kite', and the two sola-topee'd gentlemen as 'self and L. Allenby', 'taken just before flight to Kassala (note the sand)'. The next machine is J9809, which poses a query as to the unit concerned. While J9809 is only on record as serving with No 47 Squadron as a seaplane, J9813 was with No 14 Squadron before it was rebuilt as Gordon JR9813 and then went to No 47. Something is evidently missing in the records of one or both aircraft.

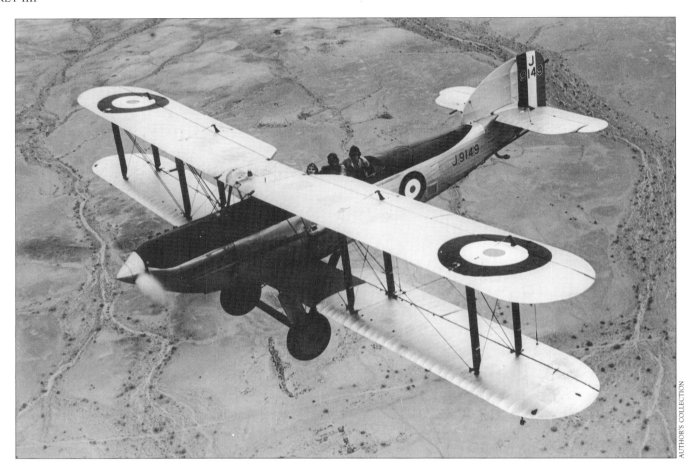

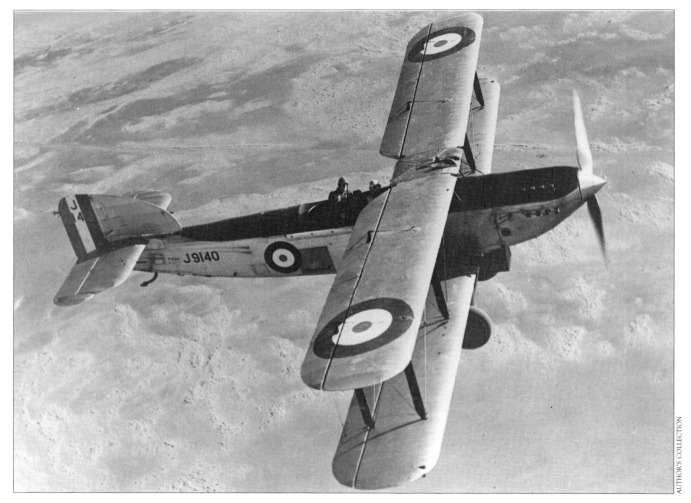

Left, upper: A pleasing study of IIIF Mk IV C/M J9149 of No 47 Squadron, with which unit it served from 21 December 1928 until December 1929.
Left, lower: Mk IV C/M J9140 served at various times with Nos 8, 47 and 14 Squadrons in the Middle East from late 1928 until it was damaged in a taxying accident in July 1931. Rebuilt as JR9140, it went to No 4 FTS at Abu Sueir, where, on 10 March 1934, it collided with stationary Avro 504N K2361 while taking off.
Right: An anonymous IIIF Mk III over the Blue Nile.

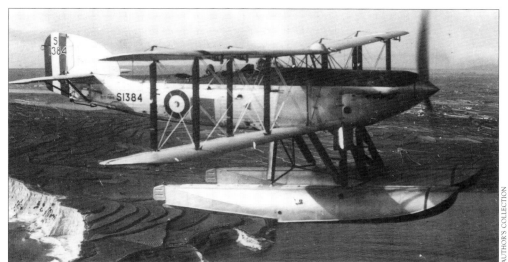

Left: Fairey IIIF Mk IIIM seaplane S1384 of No 202 (Flying Boat) Squadron, based at Calafrana, Malta, in the early 1930s.
Below: An anonymous No 202 Squadron Mk.IV at the Calafrana slipway. The red lines across the propeller blades denoted the area at the tips that was not to be held if the propeller was to be swung to start the engine, rather than using the crank handles.

Left, upper: Another No 202 Squadron machine was S1381/ '3', which joined the unit in July 1930 and was struck off charge on 2 February 1935 as 'not worth repair'. The fin and rudder of S1386/'5' are visible behind.

Left, lower: These two No 202 Squadron aircraft are IIIF Mk IIIM (DC) S1461 and Mk IIIM S1381. The dual-control S1461 also served with Calafrana's Station Flight and Practice Flight Malta before being struck off charge on 15 July 1934; S1381 remained with No 202 Squadron until it was struck off on 2 February 1935.

Below: This Mk IIIM, S1373/ '2', was with No 202 Squadron from July 1930 to August 1933, and was struck off charge on 11 October 1937.

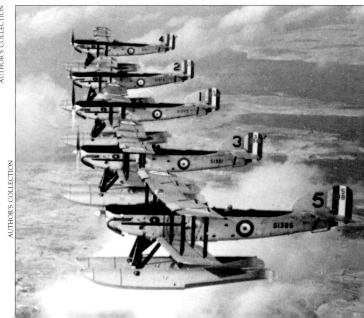

Opposite, bottom, and above: These three formation photographs of five No 202 Squadron IIIFs were not all taken on the same occasion but almost certainly depict the same five aircraft, S1385/ '1', S1373/'2', S1381/'3', S1517/'4' and S1386/'5'. The line-abreast formation flying from left to right was photographed in 1933, while the line-abreast formation flying in the opposite direction was dated 1934. In this illustration the aircraft have acquired a badge on the forward fuselage, immediately behind the engine, and this is also apparent in the third, undated view (above). Below: A line-up of six No 202 Squadron IIIFs at Calafrana, with a Fairey Flycatcher visible at the far end. The serials, from front to rear, are S1380, S1384, S1374, S1381, S1373 and S1382.

Left, top: Spot the Faireys! A 'vic' of seven No 202 Squadron IIIFs over the patchwork Maltese landscape. (Yes, seven—the starboard wingman is well out of position and has only just squeezed into the picture!) Unfortunately no serials are legible.

Left, centre and bottom: Four Malta-based No 202 Squadron IIIF Mk IIIBs on the Nile after their arrival at Khartoum in late June 1934, with radial-engined Fairey Gordon K2634 of No 47 Squadron keeping them company. The IIIFs are S1854/'2', S1381/'3', S1517/'4' and S1804/'5'. Shortly after these photographs were taken, on 28 August 1934, the Gordon drifted, hit the wall of a floating dock at Khartoum North, capsized and sank.

Right, upper: Fairey IIIF Mk IIIB S1517 of No 202 Squadron afloat. This machine became No 4 (cf. the formation photographs on pages 118–119).

Above: Tender No 160 ministers to IIIF Mk IIIB S1373 of No 202 Squadron off Malta.

Left: This No 202 Squadron IIIF Mk IIIB, S1525, seen on the Malta slipway, survived until late 1934, by which time it was with RAF Base (Med).

Below: The three identifiable IIIFs seen here with No 202 Squadron on Malta are Mk IIIMs S1385 and S1386, and Mk IIIB S1517. The purpose-designed Fairey beaching gear is evident.

121

Welcome Replacements

Royal Air Force Fairey IIIFs at Home

THE RAF at home saw the introduction of the Fairey IIIF into service in December 1927, when No 207 Squadron, a day bomber squadron based at Eastchurch in Kent, received its first Mk IVMs as long-awaited and welcome replacements for its ageing D.H.9As. It moved to Bircham Newton, Norfolk, in November 1929, where it was joined by the recently re-formed No 35 (Bomber) Squadron, which had flown its D.H.9As only for a few months as interim equipment before it began receiving IIIF Mk IVM (GP)s.

In 1929 the RAF's day bomber striking force was at a very low ebb indeed, and the Bircham Newton IIIFs, together with Andover's No 12 Squadron Foxes and No 101 Squadron's twin-engined Boulton Paul Sidestrands, along with No 100 Squadron's Hawker Horsleys at Bicester, formed the entire first-line strength. Followed as they were in 1932 by their closely related Gordon successors, these large Fairey biplanes going about their routine duties became one of the commonest sights of RAF activity to the residents of Norfolk.

Below: Fairey IIIF Mk IV (GP) J9061 of No 24 (Communications) Squadron at RAF Northolt, displaying a smart red cheat line along its fuselage. The aircraft, with the original stub exhausts, owes its pristine appearance to its rôle as a VIP Communications (DC) machine, which also explains the ample windscreen in front of the rear cockpit.

The IIIFs also enjoyed a lot of public exposure at the RAF Display at Hendon each summer. The prototype had duly appeared in the New Types Park in 1927, but in 1928 IIIFs were displayed in full service with No 207 Squadron as part of the day bomber contingent, which also included No 11 Squadron's Horsleys, No 12's Foxes and Nos 600 and 601's D.H.9As.

In 1929 No 207 Squadron made a second appearance at RAF Hendon, led by Squadron Leader E. A. Beulah, in an air battle set-piece which also included eighteen Armstrong Whitworth Siskins of Nos 29 and 56 Squadrons, five Fairey Flycatchers, ten Handley Page Hyderabads of Nos 10 and 99 Squadrons and a kite balloon (rapidly demolished). To add to the festivities, Flight Lieutenant S. D. Macdonald DFC gamely flew a IIIF in competition with a Flycatcher, a Gloster Grebe, two Gloster Gamecocks, two Siskins and a Bristol Fighter in the famous Headquarters Race event.

Above: Mk IV C/M J9146, which served with No 207 Squadron from November 1928 until January 1930, when it was converted into a Gordon.

Left: VIP transport in action: Ramsay MacDonald, Prime Minister of Britain's new Labour Government, emerges from the rear cockpit of a IIIF of No 24 (Communications) Squadron, assisted by Flight Lieutenant H. W. Heslop, at Hendon on the afternoon of 20 June 1929, after a 500-mile flight from Lossiemouth.

AUTHOR'S COLLECTION

Below: A No 24 Squadron IIIF Mk IVM displaying its squadron number immediately forward of the fuselage roundel. Seen here at Hamble with the enlarged rear windscreen, K1115 ended its life as instructional airframe 689M.

Bottom: Another of No 24 Squadron's communications Mk IVMs was K1118, which has a raised wind deflector around the rear cockpit rather than a windscreen, and the later style of exhaust pipes.

AUTHOR'S COLLECTION

AUTHOR'S COLLECTION

At the 1930 RAF Display the IIIFs of Nos 35 and 207 Squadrons appeared in a take-off formation event also involving No 12 Squadron's Foxes and Siskin fighters from Nos 29, 56 and 111 Squadrons. Later in the show they performed what were quaintly called in those days 'combined evolutions'. In 1931 things took on a light note when a veritable circus act was performed by a IIIF flown by Flight Lieutenant J. G. D. Armour, who, accompanied by Squadron Leader P. Huskison MC in the back seat, attempted to round up 'escaped wild animals from the London Zoo' (these were, in fact, inflatable replicas), the gallant Huskison being portrayed as an expert big-game hunter wielding a twelve-bore shotgun.

The IIIF's swansong at Hendon came in 1932, when No 207 Squadron appeared with the day bomber events in which the sleek new Harts of Nos 18, 33 and 57 Squadrons inevitably attracted more attention.

Although, with the arrival of the Gordon, the IIIF left service with home-based bomber squadrons in 1932, it was still to be seen going about various second-line duties, notably with No 24 (Metropolitan Communications) Squadron at

Above: S1202/'A2' of No 207 Squadron in a loose formation over Hendon during the RAF Display rehearsals in 1928. Below: Fairey IIIF Mk IV M/A J9822/'4' of No 35 Squadron—the number again prominently displayed—has a camera gun on the Fairey mounting in its rear cockpit and sports its call-sign on the engine panelling. This aircraft ended its days as ground instructional airframe 697M.

Left: Another 'A2' of No 207 Squadron was Mk IV C/M J9147/'A2', seen here with Mk Is S1184/'A4' and S1182/'A3' behind.

AUTHOR'S COLLECTION

AUTHOR'S COLLECTION

AUTHOR'S COLLECTION

Northolt. This unit's IIIFs, fitted with special passenger seating and other arrangements, included Mk IVC J9061, Mk IVM J9160, Mk IVM/A K1115 and Mk IVB K1749, the last two being reserved for use by the Prince of Wales (later HM King Edward VIII). Notable and historic figures who used these special customised VIP IIIFs included Sir Philip Sassoon (Under-Secretary of State for Air), Prime Minister Ramsay Macdonald and Lord Londonderry (Air Minister). The Prince of Wales was once 'intercepted' in a IIIF by Siskin fighters during 1930 Air Exercises (an incident widely reported by the press), and Lord Londonderry, notoriously, once arrived at the Geneva Disarmament Conference of 1932 in a No 24 Squadron IIIF, which political agitators described as a 'bomber aircraft'.

Like the de Havilland D.H.9A, which it largely replaced, the IIIF was never given a name in RAF service, nor did it acquire any affectionately bestowed sobriquet as did the historic 'Ninak'. However, as Norman Macmillan recalls in *Wings of Fate*, Mr Hearn, a well-known gateman at the Fairey factory who always pronounced 'th' as 'f', revealed his personal discovery about the alliterative naming of the company's designs. 'I sees they all starts with a F, like the Fairey Flycatcher, the Fawn, the Fox, the Firefly and the Free-Eff.'

The General-Purpose Fairey IIIF Mk IVBs received the serial numbers K1698–K1728 and K1749–K1788 and the General Purpose Mk IVMs and IVM/As were S1175, S1178, S1183, S1197, S1199, S1203, S1204, S1205, J9062, J9067, J9073, J9132–J9174, J9637–J9681, J9784–J9831, K1115–K1121 and K1158–K1170. Deliveries to the RAF followed one of two procedures. Initially most aircraft left the Hayes factory and were taken on charge at No 1 Aircraft Storage Unit at RAF Henlow. Aircraft destined for home-based units were then delivered from there direct to their bases. Those for overseas units were flown to the Dispatch Unit at RAF Sealand, near Chester, where they were crated for shipment to the Aircraft Storage Unit at Aboukir. After arrival they were assembled and either held for training use with No 4 Flying Training School at Abu Sueir or delivered thence to their assigned squadrons throughout the Middle East. It was also at Aboukir that most of the repair work was undertaken. Many IIIFs were rebuilt as Gordons at Aboukir, with new tail units and Armstrong Siddeley Panther IIA radial engines.

Below: A flight sergeant of the parachute section at RAF Henlow takes 'Umbrella Man' aboard a IIIF in preparation for a dramatic descent during the base's Empire Air Day display in May 1939. The dropping of a dummy to entertain the spectators harked back to 'Major Sandbags', who made some memorable descents in the earlier RAF Displays at Hendon. Seen to advantage here are the footholes to facilitate cockpit entry and the fairing in front of the opening in the rear cockpit floor, perhaps used for parachute trials. By this time the IIIF was becoming rather long in the tooth.

Opposite, centre left: Another No 24 Squadron IIIF Mk IVM, with its squadron number displayed alongside the fuselage roundel. K1117, here seen at an unidentified location and fitted with a standard windscreen, became 690M.

Opposite, centre right: A poor snapshot of Mk IVM K1160 during service with the Central Flying School at Upavon in 1931. The aircraft was retired as 1583M.

Left: It is not known how IIIF Mk IV M/A J9786 of No 207 Squadron ended up in this unhappy state, but it does show the underwing weapons carriers to advantage.

AUTHOR'S COLLECTION

AUTHOR'S COLLECTION

Sea Legs

Fairey IIIFs in the Fleet Air Arm

OF the 622 Fairey IIIFs built, 352 were delivered to the Royal Navy for the Fleet Air Arm, and it was thus the most widely used aeroplane in that Service in the interwar years. The type served in every Royal Navy aircraft carrier between 1927 and 1936, and could be seen at naval air stations across the Empire. In its twin-float seaplane configuration it was widely employed in catapult reconnaissance flights in capital ships and cruisers. As stated earlier, all of the FAA's IIIFs were three-seaters, accommodating a pilot, a naval observer and a telegraphist air gunner.

An interim non-standard development batch of ten aircraft from the end of the IIID contract, S1139–S1148, preceded the production of standard IIIF Mk Is for the Navy. These were delivered to Gosport in the winter of 1926/27 and used for training, some later being transferred to home-based RAF units. As described previously, one machine from this batch, S1147, went back to Hayes to be turned into the first two-seat general-purpose version, and S1148 was used for deck-landing trials on board HMS *Furious* in 1927.

The standard production Mk Is, S1168–S1207, had the Napier Lion VA and were of composite construction. The first of these aircraft made its maiden flight

at Northolt on 18 February 1927, piloted by Captain Norman Macmillan. On 18 August that year Macmillan took the first IIIF Mk II, S1208 with a Lion XI, for its first flight, again from Northolt. This version, too, was of composite construction, and 33 examples, numbered S1208–S1227 and S1250–S1262, were built. Some were later converted to metal-winged IIIMs (see below). The completed Mk Is and IIs were held in storage at naval units in 1927, and IIIFs did not begin to enter operational service with the FAA until 1928.

The change from composite to all-metal construction came with the Mk IIIM, in which the wings had corrugated drawn-tube spars to which the pressed ribs were clipped. The prototype for this mark was the modified second IIIF, N225, which first flew in this form on 2 March 1927. The Lion XIA was introduced on this mark, and this remained the standard power unit for all subsequent FAA IIIFs. The Service's IIIF Mk IIIMs received the serial numbers S1169, S1182, S1184, S1189, S1196, S1211, S1213, S1256, S1303–S1356, S1370–S1408 and S1454–S1463, the last ten-aircraft batch being fitted with dual-control conversion sets. The first production Mk IIIM, S1303, made its maiden flight on 19 March 1929.

The next all-metal variant, the IIIF Mk IIIB, was the last Fleet Air Arm IIIF variant. Its fuselage was strengthened for catapulting, and several other detail changes were incorporated. Fairey test pilot Flight Lieutenant Chris Staniland flew the first of these aircraft, S1474, on its maiden flight on 6 June 1930, from Northolt (or possibly from Fairey's new aerodrome at Harmondsworth). In all,

Below: After serving with 443 Flight in HMS *Furious* as '36', Mk I S1189 joined 445 Flight in *Courageous*, retaining the same side number.

Right: The last of the batch of ten non-standard development IIIFs, modified from IIIDs on the production line, 'Interim Type' S1148 has the original IIID-type vertical tail surfaces and a standard Scarff ring for the rear-cockpit gun.

166 were delivered to the Royal Navy, numbered S1474–S1552, S1779–S1844 and S1845–S1865, the last example being delivered on 10 September 1932. Two, S1845 and S1851, were dual-control versions.

On its entry into FAA service in 1927 the IIIF replaced the IIID in 440 Flight and was the initial equipment of 445 and 446 Flights. Two years later it replaced the Avro Bisons of 447 and 448 Flights, and 441 Flight's Fairey IIIDs. In 1931 the Blackburn Blackburns of 449 and 450 Flights made way for IIIFs, and in 442 and 444 Flights it replaced the FAA's last remaining IIIDs. The last unit to receive the IIIF was 460 Flight in *Glorious*, which had its Blackburn Ripons replaced in November 1932.

When the FAA Flights were merged from April 1933 to create squadrons, five spotter-reconnaissance squadrons had Fairey IIIFs. These were 820 Squadron (formed from 450 Flight), 822 Squadron (from 442 and 449 Flights), 823 Squadron (from 441 and 448 Flights), 824 Squadron (from 440 and 460 Flights) and 825 Squadron (formed on 8 October 1934 by renumbering 824 Squadron in HMS *Eagle*).

Although the IIIF was largely supplanted by the radial-engined Fairey Seal in 1934, it continued to serve with 822 Squadron on board *Furious* and 825 Squadron in *Glorious* until 1936.

Below: Another view of 'Interim Type' S1148. After being used for press demonstrations, the aircraft undertook deck-landing trials on board *Furious* in 1927 and carried out catapult trials at RAE Farnborough from 29 July that year.

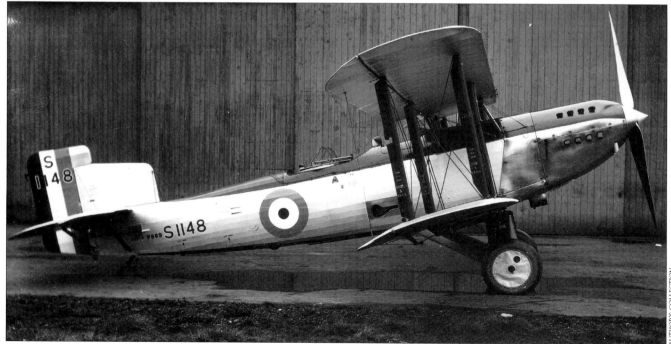

In the era of the IIIF the arrester-wire system had not yet been adopted on board Royal Navy aircraft carriers, so the type was not fitted with any form of arrester hook. However, one aircraft, S1781, was used by the RAE's Experimental Flying Department in the first controlled experiments with a rear-fuselage deck hook of the kind later standardised on Seals, Ospreys and other biplanes. This comprised a swinging triangular steel frame with a spring-loaded hook at its apex, which was held flush with the fuselage underside in normal flight but could be lowered by the pilot when required. Following initial trials with arrester wires laid on Farnborough airfield, the first shipborne trials were made in *Courageous* in 1931, using the new athwartships arrester wires in place of the earlier longitudinal restraining wires designed to be engaged by claws on the aircraft's undercarriage spreader bars. Connected to under-deck hydraulic 'jiggers', the wires were paid out as the aircraft's hook snatched one.

Above: The first production IIIF Mk IIIM, S1303, made its first flight on 19 March 1929, shortly before this photograph was taken. The aircraft subsequently flew with 447 Flight on board *Furious*, with the side number '40', and then with 442 Flight in *Furious* and *Courageous* as '136'.

In its seaplane form the catapult-stressed IIIF Mk IIIB was issued to warships, serving in this role for several years until it was replaced by the Osprey. Eight were allocated to the cruiser HMS *York*, five to the cruiser *Exeter* and two to the battlecruiser *Hood*, while the cruisers *Norfolk* and *Dorsetshire* and the battleship *Valiant* had one each. Seaplane IIIFs were also used on aircraft carriers' catapults, including those of *Hermes* and *Glorious*. At RAE Farnborough, IIIF Mk III seaplane S1317 was used for catapult launch experiments. This same machine, among several others, was also used for trials with the Catapult Flight at Leuchars.

One of the IIIF crews' regular duties was spotting for the battleships' big guns during target practice. The target comprised a canvas and lattice framework mounted on a hull designed to leave a conspicuous wash when towed—using a healthy length of cable—behind a tug. The ships' gunners would fire at the target

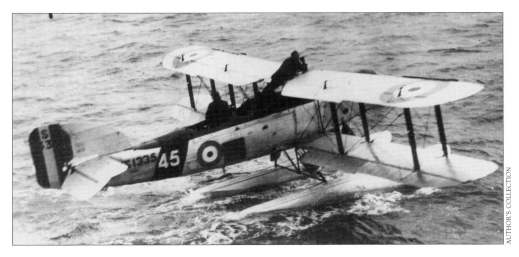

Left: Fairey IIIF Mk IIM S1335/'45' was with 441 Flight on board HMS *Argus* from March 1929, but crashed on alighting on 20 September 1929 and sank. Recovered two days later, it then joined the Coast Defence Co-operation Flight at Eastchurch, and subsequently served in *Courageous*. The fuselage serial number was sometimes repositioned, as seen here, in order to keep it clear of the coloured band.

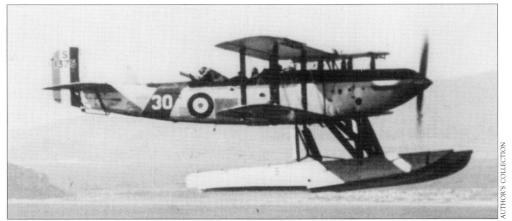

Left: Seen here off Gibraltar, Mk IIIM S1375/'30' was with 441 Flight on *Argus* until February 1930, when its Flight transferred to *Glorious*. In 1933 it was with 823 Squadron on the latter ship. It was standard practice within the FAA to identify an aircraft's parent carrier by means of a raked coloured band across the fuselage; that for HMS *Argus*, as here, was green.

Left: Another Mk IIIM of 441 Flight in *Argus*, S1330/'40' is reported to have crashed while landing in 1929. After surviving several firings as a catapult dummy from *Ark Royal*, it capsized on 1 May 1930, the wreckage being hoisted aboard at Spithead.

from a position which, according to Group Captain Peter Heath, 'seemed to be over the horizon'. While this was in process the spotter aeroplane 'hung about in what it hoped was a safe place, reporting the fall of shot'. He continues:

> What was interesting was not so much the accuracy of the shooting, which was . . . appalling, but the effects. When a battleship fired a salvo of four guns, the recoil pushed the whole vast bulk of the ship sideways through the water and, for a long time afterwards you could see the kink in its otherwise straight wake, showing where it had actually fired. Simultaneously, the surface of the sea in a wide segment in front of the guns would be pressed completely flat. All waves would temporarily vanish over an area which must have spread out a quarter of a mile from the ship. Gradually they would return, from the ship outwards.
>
> If you were behind the guns and not too high (a safe place but not the best for observation), you could sometimes see the shells leave the guns and follow their flight. Not surprisingly, really, since they weighed over a ton each. On a short-range shoot, with a flat trajectory, shells might ricochet on hitting the water instead of plunging in, and you saw these enormous lumps of metal cartwheeling off into the distance for heaven knows how far. Part of our responsibility was to watch for and report anything that wandered into the 'outfield'.

At Gosport, IIIFs were used to train telegraphist air gunners, while naval observers underwent their training on IIIFs at the School of Naval Co-operation at Lee-on-Solent.

While the FAA's IIIFs were principally intended to serve in the spotter-reconnaissance role, being the last representatives of this class along with the Seals, they could also be used for precision high-bombing attacks against enemy fleets. However, the Admiralty never took this tactic very seriously. Surprisingly, the FAA's IIIFs were not declared obsolete until early in 1940. Some remnants of a former Naval IIIF are in the custody of the FAA Museum at Yeovilton.

Above: Three IIIFs of 820 Squadron in *Courageous* on patrol, probably in 1933. On the right is Mk IIIB S1492/ '749', in the centre is Mk II S1211/'748' and on the left is Mk IIIM S1354/'745'. All three aircraft had quite long lives with a variety of units.
Right: A trio of Mk IIIBs of 446 Flight on board *Courageous*—(front to rear) S1546/'734', S1499/'730' and S1498/'735'. The coloured bands are in this instance blue.

Left: A crew member sits on the upper wing centre section of IIIF Mk IIIM seaplane S1334/'27' of 441 Flight (HMS *Argus*), waiting to attach the strop to the crane that will hoist it back on board. A repositioned fuselage serial number is again noteworthy; on some FAA aircraft it was omitted altogether.

Right: Another seaplane of 441 Flight in *Argus*, S1330 (call-sign '40' in serial records, though the code looks different here), taxies away with a crew member standing on the sides of the pilot's cockpit while he stows away the strop—a precarious-looking procedure.

Left: Seen at the top of the slipway at Calafrana, Malta, IIIF Mk II S1224/'42' was with 445 Flight in *Courageous*. Its sad end is recorded in later photographs—see page 144.

Right: Fairey IIIF Mk II S1250/'46' was with 445 Flight in *Courageous*, and was later converted to a seaplane and suffered a mishap while alighting (see pages 142–143).
Below : Three IIIFs of 446 Flight in *Courageous* flying over Malta about 1930—Mk II S1223/'39', Mk III S1307/'40' and Mk II S1210/'42'. The differing fin markings are of interest, and all the aircraft have blue upper wing surfaces and blue fuselage top decking in the carrier's colour. The interplane jury struts normally fitted only when the wings were folded are still in place.

Right: A study of IIIF Mk III S1307/'40' of 446 Flight from HMS *Courageous*. The chequered tailplane and elevators are noteworthy.

Below: Another view of the three IIIFs depicted in the photograph opposite bottom— S1223, S1307 and S1210.

AUTHOR'S COLLECTION

AUTHOR'S COLLECTION

135

Above and right: Further flying studies of IIIF Mk III S1307/ '40' of 446 Flight (*Courageous*). In the first photograph roundels can be seen on the wheel covers; the large square casing partly obscuring the blast channel for the Vickers gun is the housing for a flotation bag. The fuselage sash and chequerboard markings are blue and white.

Below: Lions roaring, a Flight of IIIFs prepares to take off from *Courageous*, about 1931. The foremost machine is S1351/'32' of 445 Flight, a Mk IIIM that was written off on 15 July 1932 when it crashed into the sea off the Isle of Wight on take-off from the carrier for a flight to Gosport. Both the pilot, Lieutenant (Flying Officer RAF) G. B. Kingdon, and his passenger were 'OK'.

Right and below: Three in-flight studies of Mk II S1210/52 of 446 Flight, *Courageous*, displaying distinctive roundels on the wheel covers. The engine starting cranks are still in place (which was not unusual), as are the interplane jury struts, and the impeller-driven generator is protruding from the starboard side of the fuselage.

Right: This Mk IIIB, S1491/ '53', was with 450 Flight on board *Courageous* and was later numbered '749'. On 17 February 1932 Flying Officer G. F. Whistondale parachuted to safety when the aircraft crashed and sank off Marsa Scirocco, Hal Far, but Able Seaman J. Starley drowned (see page 70). The aircraft was apparently recovered.

Left: Next along the production line from S1210, S1211/ '41' was on 445 Flight in *Courageous*, and has stars on its wheel covers. This long-lived Mk II, rebuilt as SR1211 in 1934–35, survived several accidents until 28 October 1936, when it was written off while operating as a seaplane from HMS *Barham*. It failed to flatten out soon enough, crashed and sank in Gibraltar Harbour, fortunately without harming its pilot, Lieutenant (Flying Officer RAF) A. C. Newson.

Right: This IIIF Mk II, S1226/ '46', was with 455 Flight in *Courageous* in 1928. Early in 1931 it was used for flotation gear tests at A&AEE Martlesham Heath, and a few months later it joined the Experimental Flying Flight at RAE Farnborough.

Opposite, bottom: Although IIIF Mk I S1196/'39' was with 446 Flight on HMS *Courageous*, this photograph shows it after going off into the palisades on board *Furious*. In 1934 it joined 822 Flight for *Furious*, but on 2 November that year it suffered engine failure and its pilot,

Lieutenant (Flying Officer RAF) C. E. H. Batham, ditched it in the sea ten yards from the shore at Orfordness, overturning it in the process. Batham and his telegraphist passenger swam ashore, and S1196 went to A&AEE Martlesham Heath for tests.

Above, left: An anonymous IIIF descends on the deck lift after colliding with the funnel of *Courageous* on 5 May 1931.
Above, right: A bedraggled *Courageous* IIIF bearing side number '15' is hoisted from 'the drink' in 1930. Apparently

it sank in 30 seconds, but its pilot was saved.
Below: An S-serial Fairey IIIF prepares to depart from the deck of HMS *Courageous*. Deck handlers hold on to the lower wing of the next in line for take-off.

AUTHOR'S COLLECTION

AUTHOR'S COLLECTION

Above: A fine air-to-air study of Mk II S1223/'54' of 446 Flight, HMS *Courageous*, circa 1929–30.
Left: Fairey IIIF '746' of 450 Flight starts its take-off run on board HMS *Courageous*.

Below: Three IIIF Mk IIIBs of 446 Flight, HMS *Courageous*, over Grand Harbour, Malta. Aircraft '730', leading the formation, is S1499. The nearest aircraft, '734', is S1546, and the furthest, '735', is S1493.

Opposite: Pilot Officer P. J. H. Halahan in Fairey IIIF Mk II S1220/'42' of 445 Flight went into the palisades of *Courageous* off Jaffa in 1929. The first two photographs (opposite, top) show just how close the aircraft came to going right overboard. In the third photograph (right) the aircraft has been hauled back on to the deck.

AUTHOR'S COLLECTION

Left and right: Mk II seaplane S1250/'46' of 445 Flight, *HMS Courageous*, on 17 July 1929. While alighting in Dragomesti Bay, off Skiathos, on 17 July 1929, it lost a float and suffered a damaged lower port wingtip. Its pilot, Lt L. J. S. Ede, was unhurt.

Above: Three IIIF Mk IIIBs of 450 Flight up from *HMS Courageous*: S1492/'743' is followed by S1500/'750' and '746'.

Right: An unusual view from the flying-off deck as a IIIF takes off from HMS *Courageous*.

Above, left: This forlorn tangle of wreckage is believed to be all that remained of IIIF Mk II S1254/'54' of 446 Flight, *Courageous*, after it bounced on the ramp aft, its starboard wing hit a mast and it spun, pancaked into the sea and disintegrated on 3 July 1928. Needless to say, it was a write-off.

Above, right: On 3 July 1929, while flying from the battle-ship HMS *Resolution* as a sea-plane, IIIF Mk II S1224/'42' of 445 Flight, *Courageous*, stalled at 70 feet and dived into a hillside on Dragomesti Island. Although it was written off, its pilot was unhurt.

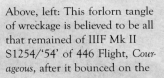

Above: HMS *Courageous* under way, with a IIIF being man-handled on deck and the windbreak raised. The lower flying-off deck at the bows—in practice, rarely used—is clearly evident in this photograph. Below: Fairey IIIFs from HMS *Courageous* lined up at Hal Far, Malta. The nearest three aircraft are, from right to left, S1308/'41', S1210/'42' and S1307/'40' (chequered fin). The fourth aircraft appears to lack a fuselage serial number.

Right: Fairey IIIF Mk IIIM S1327/'46', which served with 448 Flight in *Eagle* in 1930, displays another style in wheel-cover roundels and carries the ship's distinguishing black fuselage sash.

Below: Fairey IIIF Mk IIIM S1326/'45' was with 448 Flight in *Eagle* during 1929-1931, and also wore the side numbers '43' and '54'. It later flew from *Glorious*.

Left, lower: Another Mk IIIM, S1400/'56' was also on the strength of 448 Flight in *Eagle*. It later served on *Glorious* and *Furious*, but was lost at sea off the Isle of Wight on 7 January 1936, two of its aircrew losing their lives.

Below: Two more of *Eagle*'s Mk IIIBs, S1821/'83' and S1823/ '85' of 460 Flight. On 11 June 1933 the Flight became part of 824 Squadron as a result of the Fleet-wide reorganisation of FAA air assets.

AUTHOR'S COLLECTION

AUTHOR'S COLLECTION

Top: Also with 448 Flight in *Eagle*, Mk IIIM S1343/'57' subsequently went to *Glorious*, the Coast defence Training Flight at Gosport, the School of Naval Co-operation at Lee-on-Solent, *Furious*, and then back to the SoNC.

Above: Two IIIF Mk IIIBs of 460 Flight (*Eagle*), S1822/'84' and S1819/'81', during a spell ashore in 1932–33.

AUTHOR'S COLLECTION

147

Left: Groundcrew hold down the tail of S1821/'83' and hold on to their hats as the pilot runs up the Lion and checks the magnetos. The navigation light on the port lower wingtip is clearly shown here.

Below: Having served with 440 Flight in *Hermes*, Mk IIIB S1474/'74' then joined 824 Squadron in *Eagle*—which was then redesignated 825 Squadron. It retained the same callsign throughout.

Below and bottom: The spotlight here is on Mk IIIB S1487/'86' of 824 Squadron as it runs up on *Eagle*'s deck (with deck hands lying prone under the lower wings to hold the chocks in place) and takes off (leaving the chock-holders behind).

Right: Two studies of 824 Squadron's IIIF Mk IIIBs over their parent carrier, HMS *Eagle*, circa 1933. In the upper photograph S1487/'86' is furthest from the camera, while in the lower it has departed. The other aircraft are S1819/'81', S1820/'82', S1821/'83' and S1822/'84'.

Left and below: Fairey IIIF Mk IIIM S1326 of 448 Flight in *Eagle* carried three different side numbers at different times. These two photographs show it as '45' and '54'; it had earlier borne the callsign '43'.

Below: An overhead view of Mk IIIM S1343/'57'; the last digit of the call sign can be seen on the upper wing centre section. As photographs testify, it was clearly common FAA practice to fly IIIFs with their wing-fold jury struts—positioned close against the fuselage at the wing leading edges—still in place.

Left and below: Two further views of S1343/'57', one in landplane configuration and the other as a floatplane. The upper photograph was probably taken when HRH Prince Edward the Prince of Wales went up as a passenger at Buenos Aires in 1931, when *Eagle*'s air group formed part of a display of British aeroplanes at the British Empire Trade Exhibition held in Argentina that year (see pages 154–155).

Below: Two of *Eagle*'s IIIFs, S1343/'57' and S1400/'56', both of 448 Flight, beached in a bay, with a pair of Flycatchers (furthest from the camera) and Fairey IIID S1107 for company. At the time this photograph was probably taken, about 1930, S1107 was based at Hal Far as a landplane with the Base Miscellaneous Flight and at Suda Bay as a seaplane.

Right, centre left, and centre right: A series of four snapshots showing IIIF seaplane '52' of *Eagle* (believed to be S1370 of 448 Flight) foundering and being recovered; the destroyer in attendance is HMS *Acasta*. This machine has been recorded as 'crashed & salved on [17.7.30?]'.

Bottom: Another photograph of S1400/'56', this time with 448 Flight-mate S1320/'53' for company.

Above: With the *Eagle*'s steam streamer indicating that the carrier is headed virtually dead into wind, S1343/'57' lifts off.

Notice the lowered windbreak in the foreground.
Below: A pinnace with twelve oarsmen takes S1372/'51' of

448 Flight in tow after a heavy alighting has caused its float undercarriage to fail. Confusingly, the record states that this

machine, like S1370, crashed and was salved on '[17.7.30?]', so perhaps both '52' and '51' came to grief on the same day.

Above: Five Fairey IIIFs from HMS *Eagle* make a formation flypast over Phaleron Bay, Greece, on the afternoon of Sunday 19 October 1930, during a display put on by the aircraft from the carrier. The aircraft also made formation flights over Athens and Piraeus, and there was a 'sham-fight between two Flycatcher Chasers and a Fairey bombing plane'. *The Athens Times* reported: 'The two light Fly-catchers made some hair-raising swoops around the Bomber in their attempts to attain a pos-ition behind its tail where they would hypothetically be out of range of gunfire from the bombing plane, but in doing so, one of them came within range and the electric lamps on its wing tips showed that it was considered as put out of action. This Chaser emitting clouds of smoke with a spinning dive disappeared behind the low hills to the dismay of numerous spectators who could not follow its subsequent move-ments. A few seconds later, the Fairey Bomber was put out of

action and emitting smoke made off rapidly until it was lost to view.'

Opposite page: During February and March 1931 *Eagle* visited Argentina in connection with the huge British Empire Trade Exhibition at Buenos Aires. The carrier arrived at Puerto Belgrano Naval Base on 25 February, its three flights having disembarked on the 18th and landed at Campo Sarmiento Airfield. In addition to its usual complement of aircraft it carried de Havilland Puss Moth G-ABFV, owned by the Prince of Wales and flown by Edward Fielden, which had been transferred to the carrier from HMS *Warspite* at Gibraltar and was flown off upon reach-ing Argentina. On 4 March three Argentine Navy Super-marine Southampton flying boats escorted the Ripons of 460 (Fleet Torpedo Bomber) Flight and IIIFs of 448 (Fleet Spotter Reconnaissance) Flight to the Aeródromo de Camet, ten miles from Mar del Plata. Two of the IIIFs, piloted by Flight Lieutenant H. H. Down

and Flying Officer E. H. Shat-tock, were carrying Their Royal Highnesses the Prince of Wales (later King Edward VIII) and Prince George, respectively, who had arrived in Argentina from Chile on 1 March. Next day the Flight, accompanied by a number of Argentine military aircraft, continued on to Buenos Aires, the aircraft land-ing at El Palomar. On 7 March the princes returned to the aerodrome and inspected the machines, and on 14 March the Prince of Wales opened the exhibition in Buenos Aires. The various events to which the carrier contributed inc-luded a flying display at El Palomar on 20 March, in which Avro, de Havilland and Westland demonstration machines were flown in addi-tion to *Eagle*'s Fairey IIIFs, Fly-catchers and Blackburn Ripons. The carrier also brought a composite flight of the latest types for the FAA—a Hawker Nimrod, a Hawker Osprey and a Fairey IIIF powered by an Armstrong Siddeley Panther radial engine.

On 26 March most of the British and Argentine mach-ines from El Palomar flew in formation some 100 miles to the Argentine naval aerodrome at Punta Indio, where another flying display took place. On 4 April one hundred guests were taken by special train from Buenos Aires to Mar del Plata to witness a demonstration of flying by aircraft from *Eagle*, and on the following day the carrier arrived off Montevideo, Uruguay. The upper photo-graph shows *Eagle*'s aircraft at Campo Sarmiento Airfield, Puerto Belgrano Naval Base, Bahía Blanca. The Prince of Wales's Puss Moth, G-ABFV, is in the foreground, and lined up behind it are three Flycatchers, a Nimrod, six Ripons and six IIIFs. The three aircraft on the left are Argentine Huff-Daland trainers. In the lower photo-graph the Prince of Wales is descending by ladder from IIIF S1343's rear cockpit. Prince George is second from the right, wearing a white helmet.

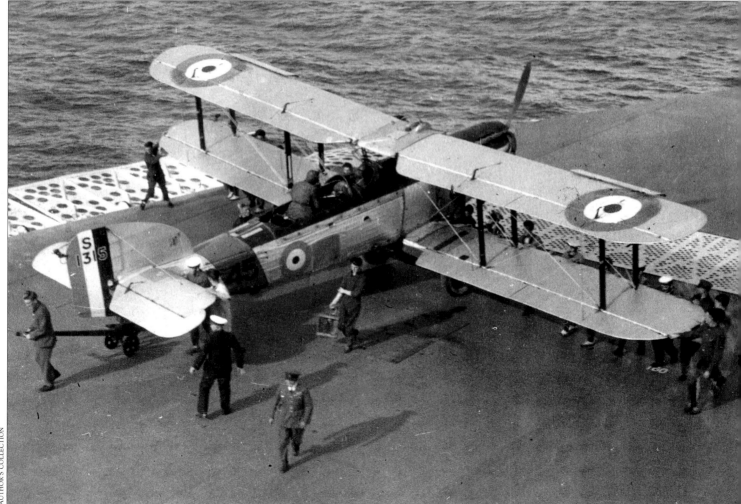

Left, upper: Frozen in dramatic poses, deck handlers watch helplessly as an anonymous IIIF goes into *Eagle*'s palisades. Right: Fairey IIIF Mk IIIM S1316/'46' noses over into the port-side palisades of *Furious* on 14(?) November 1929. This photograph clearly illustrates the 'ramp' built into the ship's forward flight deck, to assist departing aircraft in their take-off

Left: Another Mk IIIM, S1311/ '42', after becoming entangled in *Furious*'s palisades, 4 December 1930.

Left, lower: Deck handlers push IIIF Mk IIIM S1315/'45' back down the deck after a landing. Note the tailskid dolly. This aircraft is recorded as belonging to 447 Flight on *Furious*, and the diagonal yellow band bearing the aircraft's side number confirms this. However, this photograph was evidently taken from a carrier's island, and as *Furious* did not have one at this time, and the album from which the picture came had belonged to an *Eagle* pilot, it must be assumed that S1315 was visiting *Eagle*.

Above: A brace of IIIF Mk Is, S1178/'30' and S1168 or S1169/'35', of 443 Flight from HMS *Furious*. What at first glance appears to be a blind-flying hood over the rear cockpit of the nearest machine is actually two occupants bent over, engaged on some indeterminable task!
Left: Fairey IIIF Mk I S1189 or S1199 of 443 Flight in a sorry state after becoming entangled in *Furious*'s palisades.

157

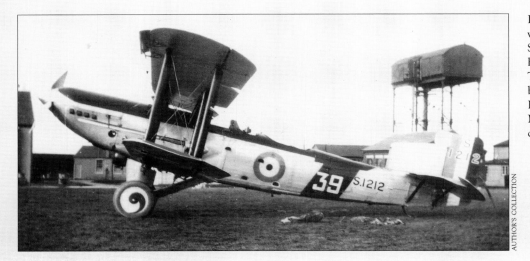

Left: Displaying some fancy wheel covers, IIIF Mk II S1212/'39' from *Furious* is seen here on 17 December 1929. The backward-sloping diagonal band was red.

Below: Well up and away: IIIF Mk I S1198/'32' of 443 Flight departs from HMS *Furious*.

AUTHOR'S COLLECTION

AUTHOR'S COLLECTION

Below: Fairey IIIFs bunched up on the after end of *Furious*'s deck. The only identifiable aircraft is S1785/'705', on the left, which was in 442 Flight.

AUTHOR'S COLLECTION

Left: Three IIIF Mk IIIBs and one Mk IIIM of 822 Squadron in *Furious*, 1933: (front to rear) S1511/'708', S1516/'714', S13??/'710' (the Mk IIIM) and S1494/'703'. The nearest two aircraft have the carrier's crest on their fins.

Below: Another IIIF Mk I of 443 Flight, S1168/'36', shows off its fancy wheel covers, 1927. The fuselage band is, once again, red.

AUTHOR'S COLLECTION

AUTHOR'S COLLECTION

Right: IIIF Mk IIIB S1785/ '705' of 822 Squadron from HMS *Furious*, in company with '742', '740' and '736' of 821 Squadron from *Courageous*. The two carriers can be seen below, *Courageous* the nearer.

AUTHOR'S COLLECTION

159

Left: Flying as '31' of 443A Flight in *Furious*, Mk I S1199 displays its diagonal red fuselage band and decorated wheel covers.

AUTHOR'S COLLECTION

Right: Taken off the coast of Morocco in February 1936, this photograph has captured IIIF Mk IIIB S1796/'906' of 822 Squadron as it banks past *Furious* during exercises carried out as part of the ship's Spring Cruise to the Canary Islands.
Below: Fairey IIIF Mk IIIM S1398/'710' of 822 Squadron from *Furious* flies over its parent carrier. While making its landing approach to the carrier off the Grenadines, British West Indies, on 7 February 1934, this aircraft stalled when fifteen feet over the round-down and crashed into the sea off the ship's starboard side. Although the aircraft was written off, its pilot, Lieutenant (Flying Officer RAF) J. O. Mansell RN, and his two passengers escaped unhurt but 'shaken'.

AUTHOR'S COLLECTION

AUTHOR'S COLLECTION

Left: An unidentified IIIF takes off from HMS *Furious*.

Below: IIIF Mk IIIM S1348, also coded '710', of 822 Squadron (*Furious*), in a photograph believed to have been taken during a visit to Gosport. This aircraft was probably S1398's replacement, as it joined *Furious* in November 1934, having previously been with 820 Squadron in *Courageous*. It later served on 825 Squadron in *Glorious*.

Below: Fairey IIIF Mk IIIB S1550/'814' of 447 Flight in seaplane guise is started up on the flying-off deck on board *Glorious* before being craned over the side for take-off. This aircraft was not a *Glorious* 'resident', actually belonging to HMS *Shropshire* of the First Cruiser Squadron. Because it was a catapult aircraft it had a plain black side number and no fuselage band. This photograph was taken when both ships were on a Mediterranean cruise that lasted from January 1933 to April 1934.

Above: Lowering S1550 over the side of *Glorious*, with its Lion running, preparatory to a waterborne take-off.

Left: An unusual formation. De Havilland D.H.60G Moth K1198/'5', Avro 504N K1956/'6' and Fairey IIIF Mk IIIB S1508/'3' were all on the Station Flight at Hal Far, Malta, when *HMS Glorious* visited the island during its Mediterranean cruise of 1933–34, and this photographs was probably taken when they flew out to meet the carrier.

Right, centre: Pursued in vain by sundry personnel, IIIF Mk IIIB S1533/'831' overshoots and goes over the forward end *Glorious*'s flight deck, 20 November 1933. At least one of the rear-cockpit occupants has already jumped clear.

Right, bottom: The pilot managed to jump clear as this IIIF disappeared over *Glorious*'s bows.

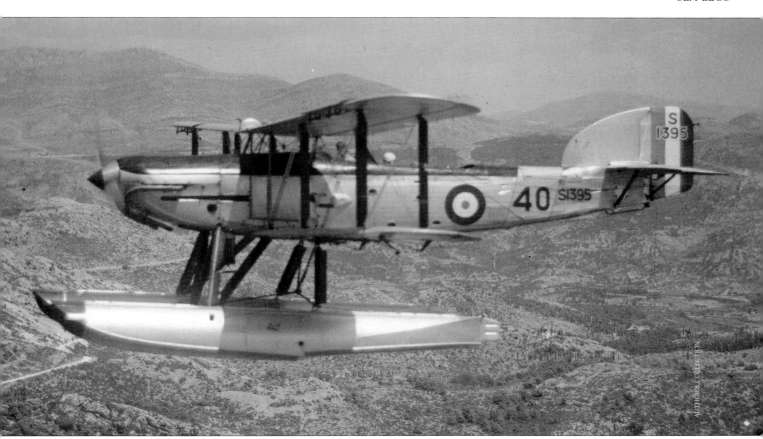

Above: Seen aloft over Yugo-slavia during the 1933–34 Mediterranean Cruise, IIIF Mk IIM S1395/'40' of 447 Flight (*Glorious*) has its side number in a yellow diagonal band, which suggests that the change of number supposedly made in January 1932 might have been made somewhat later.

Right: A moody snapshot of a IIIF returning to *Glorious* during a Mediterranean sunset.

Left: An air-to-air view of IIIF Mk IIIM S1356/'820' of 823 Squadron on board *HMS Glorious*. The last two digits of the callsign are painted on the upper-wing centre section, which, like the fin, is black.
Below: Four IIIFs with their wings folded lined up on the lower flying-off deck on board *Glorious*.

Left: Two crew members of this hapless unidentified IIIF have managed to jump clear before their mount disappears over the side of *HMS Glorious*. Deck handlers watch, unable to do anything to save the aircraft.

Right: Mk IIIM S1356 in seaplane guise when with 441 Flight on board *Glorious*. This aircraft was initially allocated the side number '36' although its fuselage band is vacant here. Below: An in-flight study of IIIF Mk IIIM S1388/'804' of 823 Squadron, HMS *Glorious*.

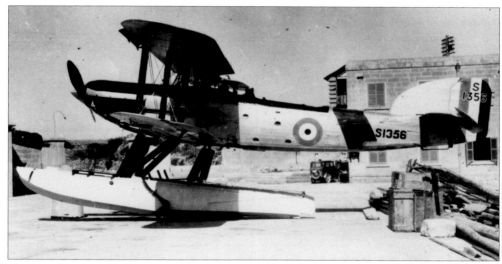

Above: Seen at Abu Sueir in 1932, S1356, now with 448 Flight, has Blackburn Ripons, also from *Glorious*, for company. The diagonal fuselage band is now wider but still lacks a number.

Right: A memorable Mediterranean Fleet occasion. During a cruise in 1932 a flypast by all of *Glorious*'s aircraft was arranged at Corfu in July for Their Royal Highnesses the Prince of Wales and Prince George, and both were taken up from *Glorious* in separate IIIF Mk IIIMs of 441 Flight on 16 August. Here the two aircraft, S1404/'801', piloted by Lieutenant Kennedy RN and carrying the Prince of Wales, and S1388/'805', piloted by Lieutenant Constable-Roberts RAF with Prince George as his passenger, formate for the camera. While 801 is flying flags from its outer rear interplane struts and a pennant from its rudder, 805 has only pennants.

Left: With the Prince of Wales aboard, S1404/'801' lands safely back on board *Glorious*. The flags on the struts were His Royal Highness's flags as an Air Marshal (port) and as a Vice-Admiral RN (starboard).

Right: Still carrying its royal passenger, S1404/'801' is struck down on the forward lift of *Glorious*. Notice the rope barrier around the lift, the tailskid dolly, and the encircled last digit of the aircraft's callsign on the upper-wing centre section.

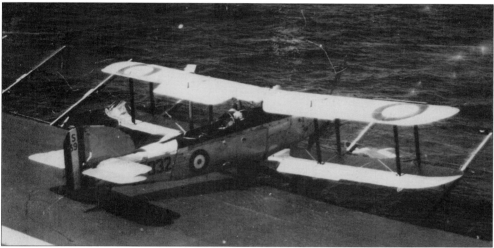

Left and below: Two photographs of IIIF Mk IIIM S1393/'832' of 823 Squadron in a *contretemps* with the palisades of *Glorious* in 1934/35 (an incident that does not seem to have been recorded). In the first picture the aircraft has just gone into the palisades, and its undercarriage is about to fall off the deck edge. The port lower wingtip has suffered particularly badly. In the second, ropes are being attached to pull the aircraft back on to the deck.

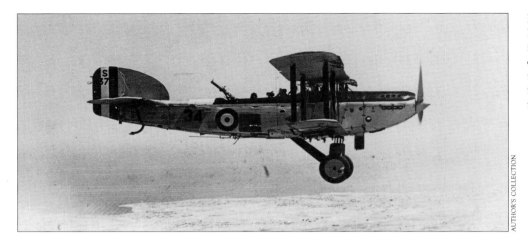

Left: A profile study of IIIF Mk IIIM S1375/'34' of 441 Flight in *Glorious*, with a camera gun on its Fairey mounting in the rear cockpit and target-towing fittings visible beneath the fuselage.

Right: Fairey IIIF Mk IIIM seaplane S1395 as '40' of 447 Flight in *Glorious* over Cyprus in 1931. This aircraft was subsequently attached to the First Cruiser Squadron in the Mediterranean in HM Ships *Shropshire* and *Sussex*.

Left: Photographed over Grand Harbour, Malta, in 1933, IIIF Mk IIIB S1510/'805' of 823 Squadron on board *Glorious* was ditched near the Gallis Rocks off the island following engine failure on 30 October that year and written off. Its pilot and Lieutenant (Flying Officer RAF) L. C. B. Ashburner RN, who was injured, were picked up by RAF marine craft.

Right: A colourful IIIF Mk IIIM, S1549/'824' of 448 Flight/823 Squadron in *Glorious* shows off its chequered fin and outlined black side number on a yellow diagonal band.

AUTHOR'S COLLECTION

Right: Flying here with 825 Squadron in *Glorious* in 1935, Mk IIIM S1346/'831' had previously served with 448 Flight in *Eagle*, and had hit the carrier's superstructure on 3 July 1930.

AUTHOR'S COLLECTION

Left: The smiling crew of IIIF Mk II S1253/'43' of 440 Flight, flying from HMS *Hermes* on the China Station, pose for their picture in 1928–29. The vertical fuselage band containing the aircraft's side number was white.

AUTHOR'S COLLECTION

Right: The crew of Mk IIIM S1356/'820' of 448 Flight/823 Squadron in *Glorious* pose for their photograph in 1932. In 1937 this IIIF was based at Home Aircraft Depot, Henlow, for use by ferry pilots.

AUTHOR'S COLLECTION

This spread: A ten-picture sequence depicting the recovery of IIIF Mk II S1252/'42' of 440 Flight, HMS *Hermes*, on 31 May 1928 on the China Station. The aircraft's pilot, Lieutenant A. O. Watson RN, had been drogue-towing, but had hit a breakwater in dense fog in Chefoo Harbour in northern China. Both pilot and aircraft were recovered, the latter very much the worse for wear. In the first picture a linked train of four rather crowded American boats has taken the IIIF in tow; in the second and third they are approaching *Hermes*.

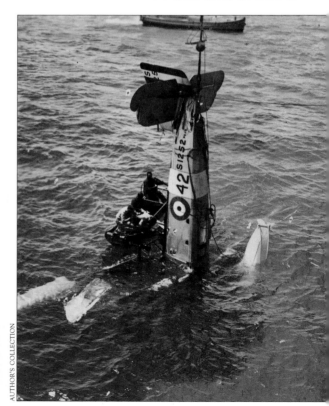

AUTHOR'S COLLECTION

AUTHOR'S COLLECTION

AUTHOR'S COLLECTION

AUTHOR'S COLLECTION

The remaining five images in the sequence show S1252 being lifted on to the carrier's deck. In the three-quarter-rear view the drogue-winching gear in the rear cockpit can be discerned.

AUTHOR'S COLLECTION

Above: A brace of 440 Flight IIIF Mk IIs up from *Hermes*. Unusually, aircraft '56' carries no serial number nor even a constructor's number, which suggests that its rear fuselage and tail surfaces have recently been repaired or renewed. The service history of the rearmost aircraft, S1215/'48', is not known.

Right, upper: Lieutenant A. O. Watson RN, was again the unfortunate pilot when Mk II S1251/'41' of 440 Flight crashed at Kai Tak, Hong Kong, in the evening of Saturday 27 April 1929. It was one of four IIIFs that formed part of a ten-aircraft formation from *Hermes* that flew over HMS *Suffolk*, on board which the Duke of Gloucester was departing for Japan. Attempting to land at Kai Tak, S1251 overshot, came low over the road and hit a tea shed on a busy corner. Although the aircraft's three occupants, Lieutenant Watson, a sergeant and a telegraphist, escaped with minor injuries and shock, three Chinese were killed.

Right, lower: 'One of our kites over the drink' is the sender's informative caption on the reverse of this image of Mk II S1255/'45' flying from *Hermes*.

Left: Fairey IIIF Mk IIIB sea-plane S1480/'43 (later '873') of 440 Flight (*Hermes*) is hoisted over the side for take-off in the China Station, *circa* 1930–32. Below: Captured by the camera just as it rises from the deck of HMS *Hermes*, Mk IIIB S1475/'40' of 440 Flight displays its chequered fin and elevators and segmented wheel covers.

Left: The same S1475/'40' of 440 Flight makes an inelegant arrival on board *Hermes*, watched by anxious deck hands. On 14 August 1933 this aircraft, then serving with 824 Squadron in *Eagle*, struck the round-down while landing off Wei-Hai-Wei, went over the side and sank rapidly. Recovered and repaired, it became '842' with 825 Squadron on the same carrier, but was written off when it again crashed over-board and sank on 18 February 1935.

Left: Hustle and bustle as *Hermes'* deck hands retrieve Mk IIIB S1479/'45' of 440 Flight after touch-down. The man in the foreground is advancing with the tailskid dolly.

AUTHOR'S COLLECTION

AUTHOR'S COLLECTION

AUTHOR'S COLLECTION

Above: Having been lowered on to the water, Mk II seaplane S1214/'40' of 440 Flight in *Hermes* starts to taxy away to take off. On 27 March 1929, while descending out of cloud over Wei-Hai-Wei, this aircraft struck trees on a hillside, crashed and overturned. It was written off, but its occupants, Pilot Officer A. G. Somerhauch RAF, AC1 G. Shaw RAF and AC2 V. H. Gillett RAF, were only slightly injured.
Left: Six IIIFs of 440 Flight (*Hermes*) await their turn to take off behind two Fairey Flycatchers in the foreground. The two nearest IIIFs have the side numbers '40' and '46'.

Left: Judging by the way some of the deck hands are beginning to run towards this IIIF—probably S1475/'40' of 440 Flight again—it is on the verge of going over the side of *Hermes* (or overshooting) after a misjudged landing.
Below: A better arrival on board *Hermes* by another IIIF, touching down with plenty of room to spare.

Right, lower: In August and September 1931, while *Hermes* was on the China Station, the Yangtze River flooded more severely than usual, causing great distress to the populace, over a million of whom were drowned. The carrier proceeded 600 miles up river to Hankow to take part in flood relief operations, some of its aircraft being used to make detailed flood surveys for the Chinese Government. To reassure the various warring factions along the Yangtze that the aircraft were neutral, Chinese messages were painted on them. Here, Fairey IIIF Mk IIIB S1478 of 440 Flight, with its Lion running, is being lowered on to the river to take off on one such flight. The Chinese-language message along the fuselage side has been painted on a strip of fabric affixed to the aircraft, and in the process of applying it the initial 'S' of the serial number has been obscured. The message, roughly translated, reads 'Life Saving Flood Disaster Committee'. The man in the rear cockpit has a surveying instrument. Other participants in these operations were American aviator Charles Lindbergh and his wife Anne Morrow, in their float-equipped Lockheed Sirius monoplane. Unfortunately their aircraft came to grief while being lowered overboard from *Hermes* on 2 October.

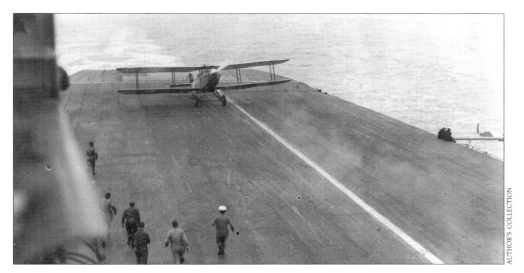

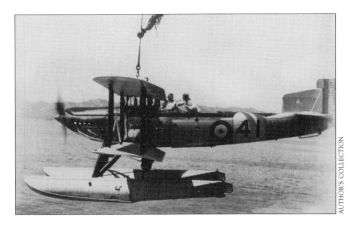

Above, left: The occupants of Mk II S1251/'41' of 440 Flight appear to be having an animated conversation as their aircraft is hoisted on to the water from *Hermes*. What appear to be markings under the seaplane's nose are merely reflections of light from the water below.

Above, right: Later side numbering is displayed on these Mk IIIBs of 440 Flight, S1476/'872', S1479/'874' and '875'. The two nearest aircraft appear to have camera guns on their rear-cockpit mountings. Below: Seen over the coast of Egypt, this formation could only have been photographed during the period March–June 1936, when all of the ships concerned were together. In the lead is IIIF Mk IIIB S1809/ '072' of HMS *Barham* (Second Battle Squadron, Mediterranean Fleet), and behind it are IIIF Mk IIIBs S1852/'769' and S1859/'780' (nearest) of HMS *Exeter* (First Cruiser Squadron, Mediterranean Fleet). Taking up the rear are Supermarine Seagull Vs A2-2/'076' from HMAS *Sydney* (then stationed in the Mediterranean) and A2-12 from HMAS *Australia* (then attached to the First Cruiser Squadron, Mediterranean Fleet).

Left: Seen leaving the catapult of HMS *London* of the First Cruiser Squadron about 1932, this is IIIF Mk.IIIB S1780/810 of 447 Catapult Flight. This aircraft had previously been used for EIIH(S) catapult tests in *Ark Royal*, and then served in HMS *Shropshire*, also of the First Cruiser Squadron.

Left: Fairey IIIF Mk IIIB seaplane S1817 on the catapult mounted on the battleship HMS *Barham*'s 'X' turret and duly protected from the elements. This aircraft served with both 443 and 444 Flights, in *Dorsetshire*, *Courageous*, *Barham* and *Furious*, until September 1936, when it went to the Royal Hellenic Navy. Below: Serving in HMS *Renown* of the Battle Cruiser Squadron, IIIF Mk IIIB S1807/716 of 444 Flight is here seen in 1935. By December of that year it was with the Reserve Pilots' Pool at Aboukir.

Below: No fewer than four different 447 Flight IIIFs borne by HMS *London* in the space of four years carried the side number '810'. Although this photograph of the cruiser at Venice is undated, the ship is known to have visited the city in late July and early August 1932 and in September 1934— which narrows down the identity of the IIIF visible on the catapult abaft the funnels to either S1405 (1932) or S1350 (1934). Both aircraft were Mk IIIMs.

Above, left and right: Two in-flight snapshots of IIIF Mk IIIB S1509/'719' of 444 Flight, which carried this side number while serving in both *Shropshire* and *Valiant* in 1933 and 1934 and then flew from HMS *Glorious* in 1935 as '842' of 825 Squadron.

Above: A rather worn-looking S-serialled IIIF Mk IIIB on the quarterdeck catapult of the battlecruiser HMS *Hood*.
Right: Another of HMS *Shropshire*'s charges, Mk IIIB seaplane S1837/'814' of 447 Flight is seen in a sorry state during recovery after it crashed into the sea in 1932.

Above: Views from port and starboard of three IIIF Mk IIIMs of 447 Flight, with the First Cruiser Squadron, over Argostilion, the capital of Cephalonia Island, Greece, during the Mediterranean Cruise of 1932. The three aircraft are S1405/'810', S1395/'815' and S1403/'812'. Argostilion was destroyed by an earthquake in 1953.

Above and right: This three-picture sequence records the recovery of IIIF Mk IIIM S1333 of 447 Flight, which was temporarily attached to HMS *London* of the First Cruiser Squadron as a seaplane during August and September 1931 and crashed in August. Its float undercarriage has evidently collapsed, and the nose of the starboard float is missing.

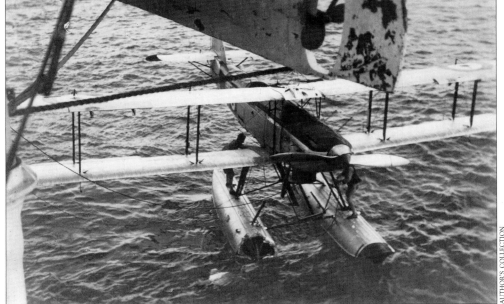

Left, upper: The IIIF Mk IIIB of HMS *Norfolk*, of the Eighth Cruiser Squadron, S1815, about to take CGS Captain Calgrove up for a flight, *circa* November 1932.

Left, lower: The same machine leaves *Norfolk*'s catapult. On 25 August 1935 this IIIF became the first aircraft to be seen by the inhabitants of the Seychelles, its impending arrival having been announced several days previously and the schools being closed for the day to let the pupils witness the event. Catapulted from *Norfolk* as the cruiser passed Silhouette Island, S1815 circled at low altitude over the capital, Victoria, several times, flew a circuit of the island, then alighted outside the harbour and taxied to *Norfolk*, which had now anchored in Port Victoria, and was hoisted aboard. Several more flights were made during the four days the cruiser was in port.

Right, upper and lower: This IIIF Mk IIIM, S1396/'B', was serving with 'B' Flight at the RAF Training Base at Leuchars in 1930.

Right, upper and lower: Two views of Mk IIIM S1347 of RAF Training Base Leuchars. The aircraft carries no individual unit identity markings.

AUTHOR'S COLLECTION

Below: Fairey IIIF Mk IIIB seaplane S1830 of 'A' Flight at RAF Calshot photographed near the Needles in 1934.

AUTHOR'S COLLECTION

AUTHOR'S COLLECTION

Right: IIIF Mk I S1186 of 443 Flight (HMS *Furious*) stalled while landing after an air test on 24 October 1929, fell into the Moray Firth and was written off. Its crew were rescued.

AUTHOR'S COLLECTION

Above: Calshot Castle provides a dramatic backdrop as IIIF Mk IIIM (DC) S1454 of the Seaplane Training Flight is manhandled down the slipway in the early 1930s.

Below: Another IIIF with the SoNC at Lee-on-Solent was S1831/'X', a Mk.IIIB that went there in 1935.

Right: Although this snapshot was reputedly taken at Lee-on-Solent, and IIIF Mk I S1188 did indeed serve there with the SoNC, it still carries the side number '38' on the diagonal red band that it wore as a part of 443 Flight on board HMS *Furious*.

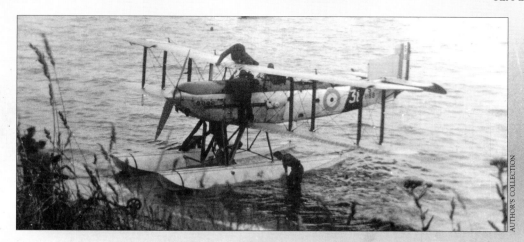

Left: A rather dark image of Mk IIIM S1348/'C' of the SoNC at Lee-on-Solent. This aircraft subsequently served in *Courageous*, *Furious* and *Glorious*.

Right: An RAF lorry delivers the fuselage and rudder of IIIF Mk IIIB S1514 to the School of Naval Co-operation at Lee-on-Solent in the mid-1930s.

Top: Fairey IIIF Mk IIIB S1794/'F', which was with the SoNC at Lee-on Solent in 1932–33.

Centre: Seen as 'B' of the SoNC at Lee-on-Solent, Mk IIIB S1828 suffered under-carriage damage when alighting in rough sea on 24 February 1936 following a navigation exercise, then sank off the Needles while under tow and was written off.

Below: Another of Lee-on-Solent's IIIF Mk IIIBs, S1543/'Y', is hauled up the ramp. Deemed beyond economical repair on 24 September 1935, this aircraft ended its days as a catapult dummy.

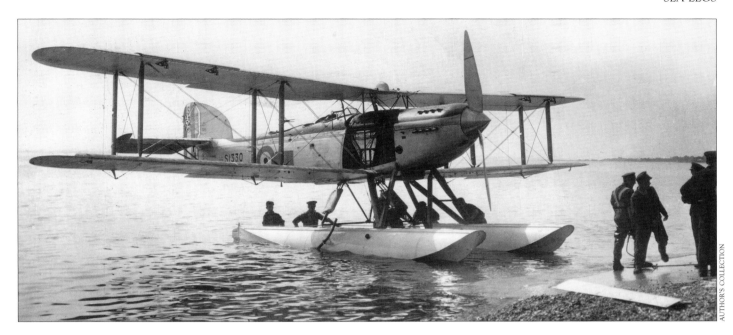

AUTHOR'S COLLECTION

Above: The recorded history of IIIF Mk II S1330 makes no mention of it spending time with the SoNC at Lee-on-Solent, but here it is. Presumably this was where it went after its service in *Argus* on 441 Flight, though it seems unlikely that 'several firings as catapult dummy from *Ark Royal* then capsized 1.5.30' would leave it very fit for subsequent use— albeit that the 'wreckage' was recovered. Notice the detached cowling panel on the beach in the foreground.

Below, left: A Mk IIIB, S1502/ 'D' was with the Training Flight at Lee-on-Solent in 1932. In October 1931, while operating in HMS *Devonshire*, it made the first airmail flight from the island of Montserrat.

Below, right: With the chevron emblem of RAF Base Gosport on its fin, IIIF Mk IIIM S1378/ 'B' of 'C' Flight poses for the camera. This machine later went to the SoNC at Lee-on-Solent.

Bottom: A pair of IIIFs at Lee-on-Solent. The aircraft on the left is S1463, a Mk IIIM that was on the Training Flight of the Floatplane Training Unit there.

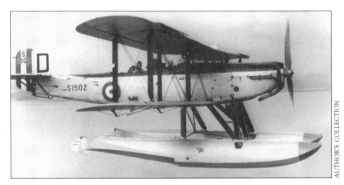

AUTHOR'S COLLECTION

AUTHOR'S COLLECTION

AUTHOR'S COLLECTION

AUTHOR'S COLLECTION

AUTHOR'S COLLECTION

Left: A trio of Gosport-based IIIFs, Mk IIIBs S1523 and S1784 and Mk I S1169, in their natural element in 1931–33. See also pages 4–5 of this book; and a picture of S1523 during its later service at Lee-on-Solent appears on pages 80–81. Opposite, bottom: Two Mk IIIBs of RAF Base Gosport, S1378 and S1501, both apparently coded 'B', aloft *circa* 1934. Above: Another Gosport IIIF that subsequently went to Lee-on-Solent was Mk IIIB S1530, which served on 'B' and 'C' Flights at the former base. Below: Gosport-based IIIF Mk I S1169 shows off the Handley Page slots on the upper-wing leading edge and the later exhaust pipe system to good advantage. The aircraft appears to have a raised fairing around the rear cockpit rather than a transparent windscreen. This IIIF had a long career both at sea and ashore before it was finally sold for scrap on 18 November 1937.

AUTHOR'S COLLECTION

In the Line of Fire

Target Tugs, Target Launchers and Fairey Queens

A ROUTINE form of target practice for the Royal Navy's gunners, be they water-based, ground-based or airborne, was provided by IIIFs fitted with air-driven windmill winches on the port side of the fuselage that enabled them to tow flag- or sleeve-type aerial drogues, or stern-attack targets. This equipment was used to provide moving aerial targets for anti-aircraft guns and machine guns during practice shoots, 'in conditions which ensure the safety of the flying personnel from injury by projectiles'. The equipment also included a type of small target designed to enable pilots of squadrons not equipped with the large targets for actual gunnery to practise interception gunnery at any time with the aid of a camera gun.

For actual gunnery practice the target was attached to the towing aeroplane by a flexible steel cable, the length of which varied according to the armament used. For anti-aircraft operations from the ground or sea a 7,000-foot cable was employed, and for machine-gun operations from another aeroplane a 1,200-foot cable was used. The target for interception gunnery practice with a camera gun was attached to the towing aeroplane by a 300-foot rope. For anti-aircraft work two types of winch gear were used, the Type A and the Type B, both fitted with brakes. The Type B was of an improved design that allowed the targets to be towed at much higher speeds.

The sleeve target, which could be four feet in diameter and twenty feet long, or six feet in diameter and twelve feet long, was in the form of a hollow truncated cone, and its height relative to the towing aeroplane could be varied by attaching a streamlined weight to the end of the cable. The flag target comprised a flat expanse of fabric fitted with a pole at the front end for towing and a net tail to give stability and prevent fraying. A weight attached to the pole was adjusted to make the target adopt either a vertical or a horizontal attitude for both anti-

Below: An apparently re-touched photograph showing Fairey IIIF Mk I S1184/'30' of 445 Flight in *Courageous* towing a 20-foot sleeve target. When the full extent of cable had been wound out, the target was trailed 7,000 feet behind the aircraft for anti-aircraft practice by ground- or ship-based guns, or 1,200 feet behind for machine-gun practice from another aircraft. If a camera gun was being used, a 300-foot line was used.

AUTHOR'S COLLECTION

aircraft and machine-gun practice. Four widths of flag target were available—ten, eight, six or three feet. There were also illuminated flag targets for practice at night. The flag target used for interception practice was small, and was towed off the ground by the aeroplane as it took off. A remote-controlled quick-release hook, usually located at the stern of the aircraft, allowed the pilot to free the target and towing rope at any time.

Designed to give a steady target for machine-gun practice at high speeds, the stern-attack target consisted of a complete cone towed base foremost. Two-thirds of its sloping surface were made from linen net, the remainder being of air-proof mercerised cotton fabric. The target was weighted by pockets of lead shot at its leading edge, the disposition of these weights relative to the air-proof gores determining the angle at which the target flew relative to the towing aeroplane's line of flight. It was carried loose in the cockpit and launched by hand.

These targets could be folded down to small size for carriage aboard the towing aeroplane. While sleeve targets for anti-aircraft practice were carried loose in the cockpit and hand-launched, for machine-gun practice they were housed in a box container below the fuselage and launched by remote control. Owing to their length, flag targets for anti-aircraft and machine gunnery (as distinct from interception flying practice) were carried outside the fuselage in long containers. They, too, were remotely controlled. The flag target containers for the Fairey IIIF were made longer than required to house the targets, extra length being provided at each end to permit location on the catapult tubes projecting from the fuselage bottom longerons.

Above: A IIIF towing a flag target during the Spring Cruise of 1931.

Sleeve and flag targets could be carried at the same time. No attempt was made to haul the targets back aboard the towing aeroplane in flight. At the end of a shoot they were dropped to the ground. For anti-aircraft operations the cable was wound in using the winch gear and the target cut adrift, but for machine-gun and interception practice the cable or rope was dropped with the target. In that case ground and bench equipment was used to re-wind the cable on to a drum for reuse.

Towed targets were used at Hal Far, Malta, and by the Base Training Squadron at Gosport, Hampshire, for the Home Fleet. A target-tug based at Hong Kong before the Japanese invasion of December 1941 was probably the last IIIF in service. Group Captain Peter Heath, with 442 Flight in *Courageous*, performed target-towing duties at Malta. He recalled:

Soon the rest of the fleet arrived; three battleships, some cruisers and destroyers all moored in various parts of the harbour. Our work was to provide targets for them to shoot at. Mostly they did this from alongside the harbour walls, the battleships particularly being very loath to put in any sea hours. So most mornings and afternoons one towing and one spotting aircraft would take off. The drogue was thrown out and the auxiliary drum of wire, about 300ft long, was paid out. This was carried out over the harbour as it was not always 100 per cent successful. If it was, the main cable would be coupled on and the drogue aircraft clambered laboriously up to 9,000ft, paying out cable as it went. This took about 40min and resulted in 7,000ft of wire hanging out behind, at the end of which

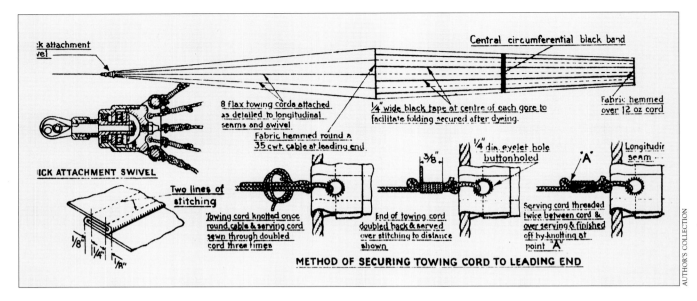

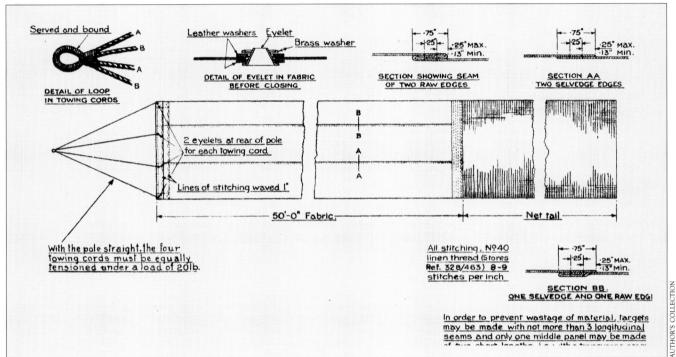

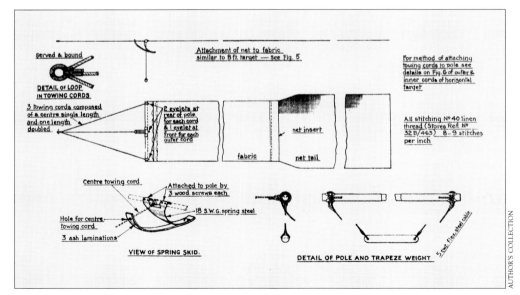

Above: Diagrams showing the construction of sleeve targets (upper) and flag targets (lower). Left: The construction of a three-foot horizontal flag target for preliminary practice.

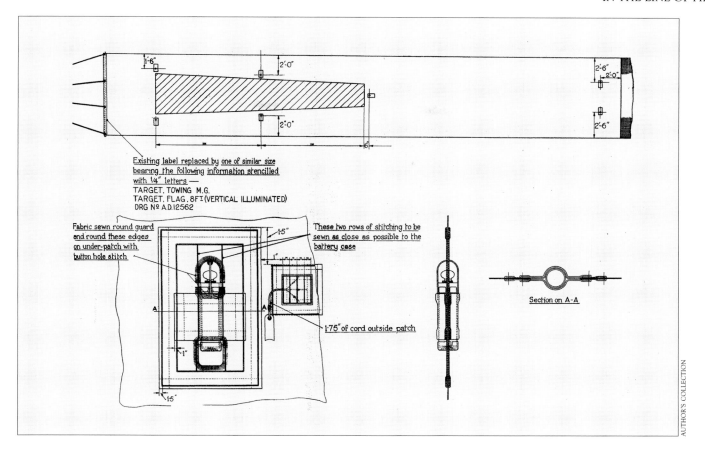

Existing label replaced by one of similar size
bearing the following information stencilled
with ¼" letters —
TARGET, TOWING M.G.
TARGET, FLAG, 8FT (VERTICAL ILLUMINATED)
DRG Nº A.D.12562

Fabric sewn round guard
and round these edges
on under-patch with
button hole stitch

These two rows of stitching to be
sewn as close as possible to the
battery case

1.75" of cord outside patch

Section on A-A

AUTHOR'S COLLECTION

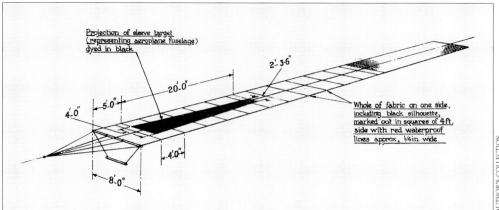

Projection of sleeve target
(representing aeroplane fuselage)
dyed in black

20'-0"

2'-3.6"

5'-0"

4'-0"

4'-0"

8'-0"

Whole of fabric on one side,
including black silhouette,
marked out in squares of 4ft,
side with red waterproof
lines approx. ¼in. wide

AUTHOR'S COLLECTION

Above: Details of an illuminated flag target for machine-
gun practice.
Left: The marking of an eight
flag target.

sailed the drogue, about 500ft lower than the aircraft. The spotting aircraft took
station immediately behind the towing seaplane and at the same level as the
drogue. The whole outfit then approached the ship at the required height, speed
and course and the guns let fly. Even with known height, course and speed it was
unbelievable how bad the shooting was and I never heard of a drogue being
punctured, let alone shot away at this game. I would like to claim, but in honesty
I cannot, that one of us was responsible for the immortal signal while drogue
towing. The towing pilot saw the first shell burst *in front* of him, immediately he
cut the cable and went home, sending as he went the signal, "Please note, I am
pulling this bloody thing, not pushing it".

After each run the drogue aircraft had to make a wide detour to get round on
to the reciprocal course. If the turn was too tight, the drogue stopped moving and
dropped and, from a lower altitude, could even hit the water, when it invariably
broke away. The drogue followed the track of the aircraft, even on a turn and,
with 7,000ft of wire out, you would complete your turn and, seconds later, meet
the drogue still cruising along in the other direction.

At its best it was a dull job and a cold one with open cockpits and no heating.
That brought problems about penny-spending. It was only later that I evolved my
own private modification of a sawn-off Brasso bottle screwed into the end of a

AUTHOR'S COLLECTION

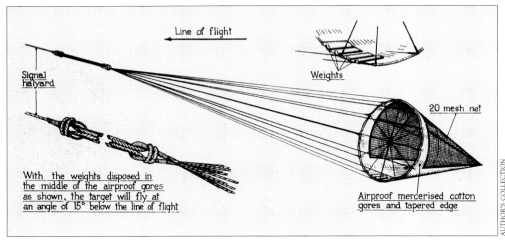

Line of flight

Signal
halyard

Weights

20 mesh net

With the weights disposed in
the middle of the airproof gores
as shown, the target will fly at
an angle of 15° below the line of flight

Airproof mercerised cotton
gores and tapered edge

AUTHOR'S COLLECTION

Above: A IIIF towing a flag
target overflies HMS *Eagle*,
about to release the target to
fall on the carrier's deck.
Neither sleeve nor flag targets
were hauled back into the
towing aeroplane.
Left: Details of the astern-
attack target.

length of speaking tube which ran from somewhere by the base of the stick,
down one undercarriage leg. (Incidentally, the humourless captain of the *Furious*
once ordered its removal as an unauthorised modification!) In those days we were
limited to passing round an empty gin bottle, which was fine for the gentleman
in the back but very awkward for the pilot, trying to maintain a straight course.

A fourth type of aerial target was the glider target, a 270-pound, 18-foot-span
monoplane glider launched by controls in the pilot's cockpit from a carrying
frame mounted on the centre-section of a biplane's upper wing. The glider had a
triangular-section fuselage and its wing had marked dihedral and a flat
undersurface and, being of thick section, no external bracing. The glider was
launched once the appropriate launching speed had been attained, and its
subsequent flight was partially controlled by means of an air-operated servo-motor
and a gyroscope of 'the obsolete spring-spun torpedo pattern', mounted in the
glider with its rotor axis athwartships, so that it was unaffected by pitching.

Once the gyroscope had been fired, the aeroplane was not to deviate more than
ten degrees from its course before releasing the glider. Upon release, the glider
would rise about fifteen feet and settle on its glide about fifty feet behind the

Left: A three-quarter-front view of a Fairey IIIF carrying a glider target.

Below: A close-up of glider target No 3 on S1789's centre section. Note that the rear cockpit has the solid-type wind deflector rather than a windscreen.

Below: The nearest aircraft in the front row of this fascinating parade of naval aircraft at RAF Training Base Gosport in 1932 is Fairey IIIF Mk IIIB S1789, with a gyroscopically controlled glider target mounted above its upper-wing centre section.

aeroplane. It was evidently thought that it would not be an easy target to hit: the description of the recovery procedure states that 'If the glider has been launched correctly up wind, it should be found floating undamaged on the water'.

* * *

In the 1920s a 'bomb-versus-battleship' controversy arose. While the Air Ministry believed that ships were vulnerable to air attack, as a result of the high percentage of hits that had been achieved on the undefended target ship *Centurion*, the Admiralty argued that, under realistic conditions, a ship's guns would prevent bombing attacks being from pressed home. At a Chief of the Air Staff conference on 2 October 1930 it was decided to undertake the construction of a full-size 'target pilotless aeroplane' that would be 'required to simulate torpedo attacks and high altitude bombing attacks' to enable the relative vulnerability of battle-ships and attacking bombers or torpedo bombers to be assessed, and that it should be produced 'if possible, in one year'.

Six days later, on 8 October, a meeting of the Pilotless Aircraft Committee was held at the RAE to discuss the best means of meeting the requirement and to develop a catapult-launched, automatically controlled full-size aircraft capable of making simulated torpedo and level- and dive-bombing attacks, and, if it survived the vessel's defensive fire, of alighting on the sea afterwards. The RAE programme was named 'Target', and it was agreed that, by using a standard Fairey IIIF and employing a catapult to launch it, a suitable target could be produced by November 1931. The IIIF also offered the advantage of being able to check the functioning of most of the equipment with a pilot and observer on board. The committee decided to proceed with production of three aircraft, the development work being undertaken by George W. H. Gardner (later director of the RAE) and J. Sudworth, under the direction of F. W. Meredith.

Using the principles previously developed for the RAE Pilot's Assister automatic control, a completely new set of automatic equipment was developed to cope with signal initiation and transmission, reception and identification; automatic stabilisation in pitch and yaw, including the ability to perform fast and slow turns in either direction; climbing, level and diving flight; and gliding at the desirable approach angle. Three throttle positions were available—fully open for climbing, partly open for level flight, and shut for gliding and diving. Several safety devices were embodied to cater for emergencies. If engine speed became incompatible with throttle setting, denoting engine failure, the aircraft would quickly adopt its landing glide condition and turn continuously in one direction until, at 1,000 feet, it would fly straight and land. In a dive attack it would pull out at 1,500 feet and automatically start to climb, and if the radio link failed for more than a few seconds it would glide down and land (or alight). Thus the aircraft was designed to respond to nine different wireless signals, *viz.*:

1. Climb at a speed of 78 knots at a rate of climb of 600 feet per minute;
2. Fly level at a speed of 85 knots;
3. Dive at a speed of 90 knots with the engine throttled;
4. Perform a 64-knot landing glide;
5. Fly straight;
6, 7. Carry out fast right and left turns at a rate of turn of up to 9 degrees per second, the turns being performed during climbing, level or diving flight;
8, 9. Carry out slow right and left turns at a rate of 1½ degrees per second.

One free gyroscope was designed to control the aeroplane through operation of the rudder and elevators. No aileron control was provided, but the wings were given five degrees of dihedral to enhance stability in a roll. The radiator shutters had automatic thermostatic control. The alighting manœuvre was designed to be entirely automatic, being initiated when the weight on the end of the trailing aerial hit the sea. It was arranged that the landing glide should be set so that sudden application of full elevator would just destroy the aircraft's vertical velocity. It is noteworthy that the automatic landings did not suffer through the omission of aileron control. The aerial was released and the gyro freed when the aircraft left the trolley at the end of the catapult's acceleration stroke. Power for operating the various controls was provided by compressed air generated by a compressor driven by a windmill mounted in the slipstream.

As had been done with other contemporary British automatic pilots, longitudinal control was obtained through the elevator by means of a gyroscope monitored by an accelerometer. This tended to put the aircraft's nose down in response to longitudinal acceleration, and to reduce this effect, which was unwanted during all pitch transitions, the motion of the throttle was caused to bring into operation a compensating torque while the throttle was moving. To introduce the same compensation during launch, the aircraft was launched in the level-flight attitude and the 'Climb' signal was operated automatically when the aircraft left the launching trolley, thus causing the throttle to open. Mathematical prediction of the manœuvre suggested this mechanism to be necessary.

Three IIIF Mk IIIBs, S1490, S1497 and S1536, were experimentally converted in accordance with Specification 5/32, being known as Fairey Queens (the name being sometimes rather pretentiously spelt 'Fairie Queen' or even 'Faërie Queen', after the style of English poet Edmund Spenser's great romantic work). In addition, two other IIIFs were loaned to the RAE's Instrument and Photographic (I&P) Flight at Farnborough for use in a number of associated trials. On 24 February 1931 Mk IIIM S1317 made the first of a series of catapult launches, and was subsequently used for radio transmission-receiver tests and wireless and instrument trials. Other radio tests and long-distance investigations were carried out with Mk IVB K1698, which was used by the I&P Flight from 12 June 1931.

Preliminary tests using S1490 in landplane configuration, equipped with the first set of apparatus but also with a pilot and observer on board, began at the RAE in September 1931. (This machine had been delivered to the I&P Flight at Farnborough as a standard IIIF Mk IIIB on 10 November 1930.) The aircraft's behaviour under automatic control, including wireless-controlled flights, was examined. One problem to be resolved concerned the operation of the automatic pitch/yaw control following a catapult launch; another was the determination of the optimum speed and height from which a successful automatic landing could be accomplished using a mechanically activated and unmonitored backward movement of the control column. It was not considered safe to test the catapult launch under automatic control with personnel aboard, so a mathematical prediction of the launching manœuvre was made. Consequently, catapult tests were restricted to three launches under the pilot's control. During one of these a maximum acceleration of 3.4g was obtained to determine whether any 'derangement of the apparatus' would occur. Likewise, it was also considered unsafe to test the landing manœuvre under automatic control with personnel aboard. However, the manœuvre was simulated at a safe height above the ground, allowing the speed of the landing glide and the height lost to be predicted. Meanwhile, the MAEE at Felixstowe conducted experiments with a standard IIIF seaplane to determine the best procedures for automatic alighting on water.

As already mentioned, in pilotless flight the backward movement of the control column or the elevator control system at the point of touch-down was to be activated by the load on a trailing weight (a 'proximeter') as it touched the surface. Successful landings were made by pilots at RAE Farnborough by gliding in at fairly low speed to a predetermined and automatically indicated height, where-upon the column was pulled back. The technique was based on the assumption that the aircraft's angle of attack could be changed from that of the glide to the three-point attitude over the same period of time that the rate of descent was being reduced to zero by one 'judicious' elevator movement. Such a landing was possible if the required rate of descent, the gliding speed and the rapidity and amount of elevator movement could be estimated correctly.

At Felixstowe the IIIF in seaplane form was fitted out as for the RAE trials and cine-camera recording was gear set up. The first tests showed that the aircraft alighted in a greater tail-down attitude than normal for a seaplane, the heels of the floats striking the water first and setting up pitching oscillations. This was not serious enough to require the angle of the floats to be altered, however, and a correct approach speed was more important than correct height if the manœuvre was to be accomplished successfully. An approach speed of 64 knots (the mini-mum for adequate control), using a 24-foot cable and full elevator movement, was finally adopted. At greater speeds the seaplane ballooned, and at lower speeds the touch-down was too heavy, but no really bad alightings occurred during these trials. Aerial weights of various shapes and sizes were tested, as it was found that the weight would break off on hitting the water if these factors were not right.

Next, S1490 was flown as a seaplane at Lee-on-Solent, where the pilot closely simulated the automatic type of landing. Although the results were deemed 'entirely satisfactory', it was thought desirable to incorporate several modifica-tions, in both the aircraft and the apparatus. Consequently a second IIIF, S1536, which had joined the Experimental Flying (EF) Flight at RAE Farnborough on 22 July 1931 as a standard Mk IIIB, was modified and fitted with the up-to-date apparatus in readiness for the first pilotless trial. This machine, which had a four-blade propeller in place of the standard two-blade unit, was flown at Farnborough during November and December 1931, satisfactory results being obtained. On 7 January 1932 S1536 was flown to Gosport and then transported by road to Lee-on-Solent to have floats and cine-camera recording apparatus fitted. The flights at Lee were made by Flight Lieutenants Vincent and Ryde, with Mr George Gardner on board as observer.

The first seaplane flight took place on 12 January, and when the automatic controls were engaged 'persistent yawing and rolling oscillations' occurred. The amplitude of the oscillations was a function of air speed, and tended towards instability at higher speeds. Unfortunately a partial engine failure terminated the flight, preventing a complete investigation of the motion. During a further flight later that day attempts were made to improve the aircraft's behaviour by adjusting the automatic controls, but only 'very slight' improvement was achieved. The main cause of the poor behaviour was considered to be the float undercarriage, which reduced the effect of the fin. Rather than increase the fin area, however, it was decided to try to cure the trouble by loading the aircraft to bring its CG forward, and making simple modifications to the control apparatus to reduce lag in the application of control.

On the next flight, on 14 January, the oscillations 'were still persistent, though of smaller amplitude and stable within the speed range required'. The tilt of the gyro axis was then reduced in flight, thereby reducing the amount of rudder proportional to bank that was normally applied, and this completely damped out the oscillations at all speeds. Various manœuvres were then performed under auto-matic control, the pilot giving the signals by operating an impulsing dial. Before all the necessary adjustments had been made, however, the pilot was obliged to descend and alight because the sea was becoming dangerously rough. In an attempt to complete the adjustment of the controls another flight was essayed on

17 January, but during take-off the starboard float became detached from the rear strut, requiring an immediate descent. Luckily the errant float swung back into position on alighting and S1536 was safely retrieved. A new float undercarriage was fitted that day.

Snags persisted. On the 19th a range test of wireless control from the ship, HMS *Valiant*, to the aircraft was attempted, but the battleship's transmitter broke down, forcing a postponement. The failed filament transformer was replaced and the range test was carried out on the 20th. Once the necessary information had been obtained, the aircraft's wireless receiver was set to give a maximum range of ten miles with the trailing aerial, but when a flight controlled from the ship was attempted no signals were received and the flight was ended. In a further attempt on the same day a number of signals were received and obeyed, but others were missed and some were misinterpreted.

A controlled flight was again attempted on 21 January, using reduced radiated power and modified impulsing characteristics. This time the signals, some sixty in all, were successfully received up to a range of six miles. The pilot then alighted near *Valiant* and the IIIF was lifted aboard, mounted on the catapult, and adjusted in readiness for pilotless flight. This work included arranging for a changeover from the main transmitter to the second office low-power transmitter to take effect after ten seconds if the main transmitter broke down, as it had done during the tests.

Unfavourable weather then ruled out any tests from 22 to 29 January, but the launch drill was practised. This differed from the standard catapulting drill, as personnel making the final settings after the throttle had been opened had encountered considerable difficulty in climbing down off the aircraft through the slipstream. It was therefore arranged to open the throttle finally using a wireless signal from the control platform, and the compressed-air system was modified to permit the changeover from the ship's air supply to the aircraft compressor to be effected after the throttle had been opened, by a person standing on a ladder laid against one of the floats. An air-pressure gauge was fitted in the fuselage side, where it could be read from the deck.

Below: The battleship HMS *Valiant* in 1933, showing the Type E1H catapult—developed specifically for launching Fairey IIIFs—on the quarterdeck.

COURTESY JOHN ROBERTS

On 30 January *Valiant* steamed to a position some ten miles south-east of the Nab Tower and took a course that gave a relative wind of 15 knots down the catapult, which was trained 35 degrees off the vessel's fore-and-aft-line. Fairey IIIF S1536 was then launched off *Valiant's* starboard side at an incidence of eight degrees with a camber setting of six degrees and at a speed of 52 knots, giving it an airspeed of 67 knots.

From observation, and an analysis of the launch film, it was concluded that the IIIF had little excess lift, as it appeared to gain only about six feet in height in the first two seconds. The aerial was released and the throttle opened to the 'Climb' position, but the aircraft assumed a bank of about twelve degrees, right wing low. Left rudder was applied by the automatic control to correct this disturbance, showing that the automatic controls were operating. The aircraft then flew on its original course, but gradually lost height and struck the sea, having remained aloft only about eighteen seconds. Its floats were torn off when it struck the sea, and it sank in fifteen fathoms before destroyers could reach it. An attempt to recover the wreckage was considered unjustifiable. (Curiously, S1536 is recorded as being with the RAE's I&P Flight at Lee-on-Solent on 1 February 1932—surely a clerical error.)

The banking of the aircraft, and the fact that the catapult's exhaust gas blew across the apparatus, indicated that there must have been a crosswind at the time of launch, but the probable drop in resultant wind speed and the sideslip resulting from the bank were not thought to have affected the launch critically. The post-launch behaviour of S1536 indicated that the means for counteracting the effect of acceleration on the gyroscope were insufficient, and subsequent investigation revealed that the theoretical prediction of the aircraft's motion, based on data obtained with S1490, had been too optimistic. It was decided to modify the system and try again.

Consequently, the third machine, Fairey Queen S1497—originally passed to RAE Farnborough on 26 May 1931 as a standard Mk IIIB and similar to S1536 in all respects, including its four-bladed propeller—was used, initially in landplane form, to determine the effect of the changes made to that machine compared with S1490. It transpired that there was a 'marked difference', partly because the change from a two- to a four-blade propeller caused a material drop in performance; moreover, it appeared that the data obtained from the tests of S1490 were 'not sufficiently accurate'. As a result, slight modifications were made to the automatic control apparatus to oppose completely the effect of acceleration on the gyroscope after launch. The necessity for opening the throttle from the 'Level' to the 'Climb' position was avoided, the engine operating at full throttle at launch. The aircraft was also given a second air compressor to ensure an adequate supply of air at all speeds in the event of leaks developing, and means were provided to prevent the catapult acceleration interrupting the air supply through surging of the compressor oil. The lateral control system was modified to give better lateral stability, which was poor when the floats were fitted. In addition, an extra wireless signal was introduced to enable a correction to be applied if the aircraft approached dangerously close to the sea during launch.

On 4 April S1497 was flown to Gosport and transported to Lee-on-Solent. After a float undercarriage and an enlarged fin had been fitted it was ready for flight on the 7th. The first flight was made on 12 April, in very rough weather. When the automatic controls were engaged it was found that the frequent bumps caused a persistent and very poorly damped rolling oscillation with 'an uncomfortably large amplitude'. It proved impossible to improve the damping of this motion by instrumental adjustments, and as the speed was varying by up to plus or minus ten knots it was decided that no useful observations could be obtained under such abnormal conditions. Later in the day the weather improved, and in the late afternoon a second flight was made in calm conditions. Although the rolling oscillation that always occurred after a disturbance exhibited poor damping, it showed no sign of becoming unstable at any speed. For this flight, attitude and elevator-movement recorders were installed, and used to obtain records during several simulations of the launching manœuvre. The 'fast turns' pressures were adjusted and the turns were performed satisfactorily, and the speed of the landing glide was met accurately.

More launch simulations were performed on the following day, and in spite of the fairly calm conditions the rolling oscillations persisted throughout the flight. The poor damping was found to be due to a leak causing a drop of air pressure, and a second flight confirmed that the damping of the oscillations was critically dependent on the air pressure but was sufficient in calm weather when the air pressure was above 30psi. During the first of these two flights, while S1497 was under automatic control, the means for applying bias to the rudder control was adjusted 'rather violently' to increase the load on the control. This caused the rudder control to go out of action, and in a few seconds the aircraft was diving completely out of control. When being flown manually a IIIF required about ten degrees of right rudder to fly straight with the engine off, and about ten of left rudder to fly straight with the engine on, and the pilot used an adjustable bias to help him in either case. However, during the automatic landing the rudder was freed and the bias adjusted beforehand to apply right rudder, to cause the aircraft to fly straight. The bias necessary to achieve this therefore opposed the control during engine-on flight, thus increasing the force required to operate the control. It was realised that, although the failure on 13 April was attributable to the low air pressure, the control was working close to a dangerous limit while executing manœuvres and correcting violent disturbances. Because the seaplane was slower to respond to its control, this effect was more dangerous in the seaplane than in the landplane.

Further launch simulations were made during the second flight that day, with different exhaust jets in the air system reservoir, and the manœuvres the aircraft was required to perform automatically were tried and adjustments made to compensate for the change from a wheel to a float undercarriage. Apart from the rather poor damping of the longitudinal oscillations during diving flight, the aircraft's behaviour was deemed 'quite satisfactory'.

Following an analysis of these two flights, it was decided to carry out more simulations on the 15th to resolve some inconsistencies, and this enabled a final decision to be made regarding the jet to be used for the pilotless launch.

Also on the 15th, Valiant arrived at Spithead, and a piloted flight was made from the ship that day. While S1497 was under automatic control from the ship some sixty signals were sent and obeyed. A range test was then carried out, signals being received 'with certainty' up to six miles. During this flight the characteristic rolling oscillation was frequently started, but the damping, though poor, was considered adequate. Further launch simulations were performed to confirm the choice of jet. Because of the rough sea S1497 could not alight alongside Valiant to be hoisted aboard, so it was flown back to Lee. At 0715 hour on 17 April S1497 was embarked on Valiant once more and mounted on the catapult. The rest of the day was spent in getting the stores from Lee and adjusting the aircraft's loading in readiness for the pilotless launch.

The sea was too rough on the following day, but on 19 April it was decided to go ahead with the launch. Again, by combining relative wind speed and catapult speed, a minimum launching airspeed of 65 knots was aimed for. The catapult was trained to fire 35 degrees off the ship's fore-and-aft line on the starboard side, and at 0800 hours S1497 was launched into a fifteen-knot wind at an incidence of eight degrees and with a camber setting of 5½ degrees. The catapult speed was 54 knots, making the probable airspeed at launch 69 knots. Although the aircraft started gaining height immediately after launch, and was estimated to have attained a height of about 200 feet, its right wing dropped quickly and the aircraft reached an angle of bank of 24 degrees after four seconds, by which time it was yawing to the right at an increasing rate. The turn was partly checked after twelve seconds, but after eighteen it started losing height rapidly until, 25½ seconds after launch, it dived almost vertically into the sea. The crews of two RAF speedboats attached a line to the wreckage, which the accompanying destroyer towed alongside *Valiant* for recovery.

After the wreckage had been examined on board *Valiant* and at Gosport, S1497's engine and fuselage were returned to the I&P Flight at the RAE for further examination. The gyroscope had been almost completely wrecked by the heavy wireless selector gear, which had become detached from its mounting when the aircraft hit the sea. No evidence was found of any inconsistent behaviour of the automatic controls, but it was concluded that 'a remarkable series of events had occurred after the aircraft struck the sea'. The throttle was found to be nearly shut, and the mechanism which performed the alighting manœuvre had operated. When S1497's propeller had hit the sea, the consequent slowing down of the engine must have activated the 'Engine failure' control, thus operating the landing glide signal through the selector gear and closing the throttle. Because the landing glide signal was operating, this permitted the trailing weight to operate the actual landing signal and switch off the engine. Although the compressed-air supply must have failed before the throttle was completely closed, the air pressure must have been at least some 15psi when the aircraft hit the water. After the apparatus had been removed from the wreckage, dismantled and cleaned to arrest seawater corrosion, the selector gear was found to be in complete working order without requiring any adjustment. About half of it was reusable if needed.

The possible causes of the failure were considered, and it was concluded that it was probably due to the inability of the rudder control to respond quickly enough to check the post-launch disturbance. The rudder was extremely heavy, and wind-tunnel tests confirmed that the IIIF seaplane's poor lateral control could be ascribed to a deficiency in weathercock stability compared with the landplane owing to the effect of the floats (which of course had not been fitted during the initial tests at Farnborough). 'It is therefore desirable,' the resulting report concluded, 'that a more powerful and aerodynamically balanced rudder should be employed on the next aircraft.' Surprisingly, S1497 survived, and was at Gosport on 28 February 1933.

Having decided that an attempt should be made to improve control of the aircraft to cope with the disturbances likely to arise during catapulting and by the bursting of shells, the RAE arranged that the first Fairey Queen, S1490, now duly modified to conform with its two unfortunate sisters, be fitted with a specially designed, more powerful and aerodynamically balanced 'all-moving' rudder. Wind-tunnel tests had shown that this new rudder should be more powerful and give more stable lateral control than the standard fin and rudder. In addition, the automatic control was made more powerful by increasing the air pressure by 25 per cent, and the range of the rudder control was increased. However the new rudder would impose greater torsional loads on the aircraft's fuselage, and to satisfy airworthiness requirements a device had to be installed to prevent the automatic control from applying excessive amounts of rudder. It was arranged that this device could be deactivated for a pilotless flight. To improve reliability, standard automatic telephone electromagnets were adopted to operate the fourteen air valves, and an air reservoir was fitted to smooth out any variations in pressure that might occur, as, for example, during launch.

Because the previous failures had primarily been brought about by catapulting, and many successful flights under complete radio control had been made after the aircraft had been flown to a suitable height by a human pilot, on 23 June 1932 the Air Ministry—under political pressure to ensure that the remaining Fairey Queen could be used as a target—suggested to the Admiralty that the aircraft should not be catapulted, and that a human pilot should fly it to a safe height and then bale out before gunnery trials started with the aircraft under wireless control. Preparations were therefore made to fit a ladder to facilitate the pilot's exit. The pilot originally selected for this unenviable task, Flight Lieutenant J. A. T. Ryde, was injured in a practice parachute jump at Henlow, and a substitute was chosen. He underwent some tests in the Aldershot Command Swimming Baths to determine whether or not a parachutist could swim clear if he were enveloped by his parachute, and to investigate the functioning of the quick-release gear under these conditions. After considerable discussion, however, the idea was abandoned, and on 17 August 1932 the RAE was informed that the aircraft should be catapulted after all, but with no gunnery trials on the first occasion. Meanwhile, it had been expected that the new rudder would be available by mid-July, and that it would be possible to transfer S1490 to Lee-on-Solent early in August and complete the flight tests by the end of the month. Thus it was hoped that the aircraft would be ready for the third shipborne pilotless launch by 1 September.

The first flight of Fairey Queen S1490 in its modified configuration took place on 9 August 1932. The new rudder was found to be both lighter to operate and more powerful than the standard IIIF rudder under both engine-on and engine-off

Below: The increased dihedral of the wings of the Fairey Queen unmanned, remote-controlled aerial target are evident in this picture of the second of the three conversions, IIIF Mk IIIB S1536, on HMS *Valiant*'s catapult in January 1932. The one and only launch of this aircraft from *Valiant* resulted in a flight of a mere eighteen seconds before S1536 struck the sea, insufficient means having been provided to counteract the effect of acceleration on the gyroscope that controlled the aircraft through the operation of its rudder and elevators.

conditions. A much smaller rudder angle was required in order to fly straight and level, and the aircraft's lateral stability under automatic control was 'much improved'. Two more wireless-controlled flights were made to test the general functioning of the apparatus, and, the results being satisfactory, S1490 was flown to Gosport on 18 August and then transported to Lee-on-Solent by road.

After a float undercarriage had been fitted, S1490 flew in seaplane form on 23 August. Both pilots who had previous experience with the standard rudder on a IIIF seaplane pronounced the new rudder a great improvement, and said that the aircraft was much easier to fly. Several flights were made during the following week to test general manoeuvrability under automatic control, and to simulate as far as possible the launching and alighting manoeuvres. The alighting simulations were performed by operating the landing signal, while under automatic control, at a safe height. Records of air speed and acceleration were taken, to determine the best speed for the glide and the distance required between the trailing weight and the floats.

On 31 August *Valiant* arrived at Spithead, and, following a successful ground test transmission at a range of 4½ miles, a test flight under wireless control was attempted that morning. It proved a failure, only a few of the signals sent being received correctly. The aircraft returned to Lee, and it was determined that *Valiant*'s transmitter was faulty. After a week of ground testing the source of the trouble was pinpointed and a high degree of reliability was achieved, and on 7 September the decision was made to attempt a further flight as soon as weather permitted and to conduct range tests on both the ship's main wireless office and the second office transmissions. Thus, on 9 September, two flights were made, and all signals from the main office were correctly received. It transpired that a range of at least 12½ miles could be obtained with the main transmitter without serious overloading close to the ship, but that the second office transmitter gave a 'doubtful range' of only half a mile and its signals were occasionally misinterpreted. Consequently, any hope of using the second office as a standby was abandoned.

At 1500 hours on 9 September S1490 was embarked on *Valiant*, and the 10th was spent preparing the Fairey Queen for launch. Bad weather over the ensuing few days precluded a launch, and they were spent on practice drills. This time, because the aircraft had been subjected to considerable lateral disturbance on the previous two trials, greater attention was paid to determining the strength and direction of the natural wind. A long pennant was attached to the top of the mast, and the wind speed indicator was mounted twelve feet above one of the after gun turrets. Owing to previous difficulties in defining control-surface movements after launch by analysing film taken from the ship, simple scales and pointers were fitted to S1490's elevator and rudder and photographed by a Pathescope cine camera mounted on the aircraft's top wing centre section. The camera was set to be started by the acceleration during launch.

On 14 September the weather promised to be suitable, so *Valiant* weighed anchor at 0800 hours. While the ship was proceeding to an area south-east of the Isle of Wight, her aircraft sent a weather report from the area, stating that the wind strength was five knots, that the sea was unsuitable for alighting, and that the height of the lowest clouds was between 2,000 and 2,500 feet. A three-foot swell was running when *Valiant* reached the area, but it was decided to 'pre-launch' S1490 and proceed with the launch if the wind speed did not decrease.

The pilotless Fairey Queen S1490 was launched at noon, the catapult instruments indicating a speed of 54.3 knots and a maximum acceleration of 2.9g. The mean wind speed was sixteen knots, and was straight down the catapult, which was again trained 35 degrees to starboard. No noticeable disturbance occurred,

except that the starboard wing dropped about seven degrees and the aircraft yawed slightly to port.

As the aim was to test the launch and alighting, the flight was kept as brief as possible. The machine's reliability in flight under wireless control had been tested for many hours at Farnborough and Lee-on-Solent with a pilot on board, and the 'apparent unreliability' of *Valiant*'s transmitter further justified curtailment of the flight. The aircraft was allowed to fly straight and climb for 55 seconds, when the 'Fast right turn' signal was transmitted and received correctly. It was then climbed to about 2,500 feet, being kept well within wireless range by sending occasional signals to turn. While flying level and performing a fast right turn at that altitude S1490 entered a cloud and was lost from sight for a few seconds. It was then manœuvred until it was flying approximately into wind, when the 'Landing glide' signal was sent. Only very slight disturbances in roll were observed during the glide, suggesting that atmospheric conditions were reasonably steady. The alighting was made 800 yards from *Valiant*, and was therefore difficult to observe in close detail. Observers saw the splash as the trailing weight struck the water, followed by a larger splash as the floats hit the sea. The seaplane bounced, stalled during the bounce, and again struck the sea. The flight had lasted nine minutes.

Valiant's whaler then towed S1490 alongside the ship and the seaplane was hoisted inboard and remounted on the catapult. It was found that its front under-carriage struts had been broken and that the bolts attaching the rear struts to the floats were also broken. Slight damage had been caused to the propeller and the undercarriage fittings on the fuselage, but none of S1490's fuselage members were overstrained. It proved possible to fit new struts and tow the aircraft to Lee-on-Solent on its own floats that evening. It was returned to the RAE by road the next day.

Subsequent analysis of the flight revealed that the speed of the aircraft at launch was 69 knots, and 87 when the 'Fast right turn' signal was sent. These speeds were considered 'reasonable'. The film taken by the onboard Pathescope camera clearly showed the elevator and rudder movements during the first minute of the flight and defined the steadiness of the launch, no control surface movement of any consequence being detected. The rate of descent for alighting was estimated from a film of the alighting at 21 feet per second, the floats were seventeen feet above the surface when the weight splashed in the water, and the elevator was 'well up' 0.3 seconds after the weight splash was seen. Because the elevator control on the IIIF was such that, even when the rate of descent was checked the aircraft was still rotating in pitch, a gliding speed slower than the best from the point of view of 'flattening out' had been deliberately chosen to prevent the aircraft from reaching an excessive attitude before striking the water. However, the rate of descent indicated by the film was deemed unsafe.

Subsequent flight tests made with S1490 on a wheeled undercarriage and without any interim adjustment of the automatic control confirmed the speed to

Above, left and right: These grainy, poor-quality but unique movie stills, taken from a printed reproduction of film shot from HMS *Valiant*, depict the successful automatically controlled catapult launch and flight of Fairey Queen S1490 on 14 September 1932. In the rear view of the launch the marked dihedral of the wings is conspicuous.

which the glide was set as 62 knots, and a more accurate determination of the rate of descent yielded a value of 18½ feet per second—though the float undercarriage might have caused a slight difference. It was concluded that the seaplane's excessive rate of descent, combined with the state of the sea, accounted for the heavy alighting. Nonetheless, the RAE had succeeded in producing a full-size aeroplane able to simulate bombing and torpedo attacks, and it had been successfully catapulted from a ship and flown as a pilotless aeroplane by wireless control.

Regarding further developments, the RAE considered that it would be possible to perform automatic landings in future with a reasonable degree of safety if the sea and atmospheric conditions were calm and if it were given the opportunity to carry out a complete investigation of the landing manœuvre. It was claimed that most of this could be done using the landplane, but that it would be desirable to confirm the results with the seaplane. A new landing weight was to be provided to ensure that the automatic signal was received with the minimum of lag, and a few flights would be made at 10,000 feet to obtain practice in controlling the aircraft from the ground. Although a minimum natural wind speed of 8½ knots had been insisted upon in previous trials to avoid any crosswind during the launch, it was felt that this limit might gradually be reduced in further trials. 'When these tests have been completed,' the RAE report concluded, 'the aircraft may be fitted with floats and used when required by the Admiralty as an aerial target.'

Thus it was that, on 14 December 1932, S1490 was ferried from Farnborough to Gosport and, fourteen days later embarked on board the carrier HMS *Courageous* in Portsmouth Dock. On 2 January 1933 the carrier sailed for Gibraltar, where the Fairey Queen was offloaded and picketed in the open, awaiting *Valiant*'s arrival. Bad weather prevented any live 'shoots' until the end of January, but on the 24th a manned preliminary flight was made to confirm the rate of descent in the glide, and on the 30th another was made to check the in-flight functioning of the automatic gear. In addition, a radio-range test involving S1490, *Valiant* and the latter's sister-ship HMS *Malaya* confirmed that the wireless equipment was working satisfactorily. Later the same day the aircraft was flown to 10,000 feet and successfully maintained level flight for an hour. A gunnery and torpedo exercise was planned for the following day, so S1490 was then embarked in *Valiant*. The event that followed proved to be a dramatic and exciting culmination of this phase of target-aircraft development, and a landmark in the history of British naval anti-aircraft gunnery.

It had been stressed that great care was to be taken not to lose the aircraft except through gunfire, and on the 31st the sea was rough and a fresh wind was blowing across the course. Consequently there was some doubt as to whether the aircraft would be able to alight safely, but the Commander-in-Chief said this was 'totally immaterial' because the aircraft was 'unlikely to survive the guns of the Home Fleet', and the exercise went ahead. It was an impressive sight as the entire Home Fleet steamed south to Tetuan Bay, where the exercise was to take place.

After launch, S1490 climbed to height, keenly observed by all below. Following the first shell bursts it began to dawn that opinions regarding lethal distance were wildly optimistic, and the seaplane continued flying, unharmed by gunfire of steadily increasing intensity. For an hour and a half S1490 flew amid a heavy barrage from the fleet, which included the battleships *Nelson* and *Rodney*, and emerged totally undamaged. It was reckoned that some 420 shells had been expended in a vain attempt to hit the Fairey Queen. After all ammunition had been spent, S1490 was throttled back and manœuvred for alighting. It is alleged that the C-in-C instructed the preparation, though not the transmission, of a signal saying that *Valiant* should not stop to collect the wreckage, as he was anxious to return to Gibraltar. However, the Fairey Queen was designed to alight

Left: Even more interesting than the previous two photographs is this distant side view of S1490 in flight on 14 September 1932, which shows the unconventional 'all-moving' rudder fitted for the final trials. There was evidently no fin at all—just a large, tall rectangular rudder—but the modification made an all-round improvement to the Fairey Queen's handling.

at the minimum possible speed, whereas most pilots did so at a somewhat higher speed. Flattening out just below the wave crests, S1490 ploughed through the tops of a few and then settled, apparently undamaged. When it was remounted on its catapult it was discovered that one float strut was slightly bent. There was no damage attributable to gunfire. Next morning the C-in-C stated that he had witnessed a miracle, and that he had been convinced of the need for more target exercises to improve gunnery, of the Fairey Queen's ability to alight in a rough sea, and of the excellent qualities of the RAF powerboat.

During February S1490 made further unmanned flights as a target for the gunners of *Nelson*, *Rodney*, *Warspite* and *Malaya*, with much the same results (or, rather, the lack of them). At a post mortem in London it was decided that the gunners of the Mediterranean Fleet, who had fared well in exercises, should have the chance to test their skills on S1490. Meanwhile the aircraft had been shipped back to Portsmouth on board *Courageous*, being offloaded on 25 March. It was then transported to Lee-on-Solent, where its land undercarriage was reinstalled. Less than a month later, on 14 April, and back in seaplane form, it was sent to Malta on board the carrier *Eagle* for a two-month detachment. Having been transferred to the cruiser HMS *London*, it took part in an exercise between Malta and Sicily in May 1933. On the second day S1490 was catapulted off *London* and reached 8,600 feet in 45 seconds. As its rate of climb was poor (owing to an engine defect) the aircraft was kept at that altitude, rather than attempt to get it to the planned height of 10,000 feet. On the Fairey Queen's first run the cruiser HMS *Sussex* fired 58 rounds, most which burst short of their target. However, during the second run at the same height and at a range of five miles *Sussex* again opened fire, and after the nineteenth shot S1490 entered a slow, flat right-hand spin and eventually hit the sea, having been aloft for 55 minutes. It sank in three minutes. (Some sources attribute the successful destruction of S1490 to HMS *Shropshire*.) The evidently high standard of gunnery gave much-needed encouragement to naval gunners, and Admiral Cunningham, C-in-C Mediterranean Fleet, was greatly impressed by the potentialities of gunnery target aircraft.

Following S1490's successful flight of 14 September 1932, it was decided not to engineer the Fairey Queen and its equipment for production, but to develop as quickly as possible a less ambitious target aeroplane which would be much cheaper and easier to handle in the Service. It was again decided to base this aircraft on an existing aeroplane which could be flown by a pilot, and the result was the de Havilland Queen Bee, the Moth/Tiger Moth hybrid that became the world's first gunnery target aircraft to enter production.

A Variety of Power

Fairey IIIFs with Non-Standard Engines

APART from the type's standard Napier Lion engine, IIIFs were fitted with a variety of other engines, both inline and radial. Two civil-registered aircraft for the Air Survey Company (see later) had 460hp Armstrong Siddeley Jaguar VIS fourteen-cylinder, two-row radials, and the aircraft supplied to Argentina had 450hp Lorraine Ed12 twelve-cylinder, broad-arrow, liquid-cooled engines and, later, cowled 550hp Armstrong Siddeley Panther VI fourteen-cylinder, two-row radials (again, see later). Trial or test-bed installations were made in a number of IIIFs. The type was the first aircraft used by Rolls-Royce as a flying test-bed, three serving in that rôle for the F.XII (Kestrel II) twelve-cylinder, 'vee', liquid-cooled engine. The IIIFs used were J9173, J9174 and N225, the second prototype, as mentioned earlier. Trials with the Kestrel-engined N225 at the MAEE in 1930 showed that although the aircraft's initial climb was better than that of a Lion VA-powered machine, the level speeds were similar and the service ceiling was 300 feet lower. During these trials it suffered detachment of the spinner and several split exhaust stubs.

The 570hp Napier Lion for the Fairey Long Range ('Postal') Monoplane J9474 was fitted as a test-bed installation in IIIF J9056. A 460hp Armstrong Siddeley Jaguar VI radial was flown in J9154, while S1325 had the same manufacturer's 525hp Panther IIA fourteen-cylinder, two-row radial. The RAE tested the Junkers Jumo 205C diesel in K1726 (see below), and Mk IVM J9150 was tested in both landplane and seaplane configuration with a 520hp Bristol Jupiter VIII nine-cylinder radial with a four-blade Fairey-Reed propeller that was installed in June 1928. The MAEE reported favourably on this combination, but criticised the heavy controls, particularly the ailerons at large angles when in use as flaps, and the liability to corrosion. Jupiter VIIIs are also believed to have been fitted to c/ns F1041 and F1042.

Below: A line-up of IIIFs fitted with an assortment of engines, photographed at the latter end of 1928: (front to rear) J9173 with a 525hp Rolls-Royce 'F' (Kestrel); J9164 with a 450hp Napier Lion; J9150 with a Bristol Jupiter radial; and one of the aircraft for Argentina with a Lorraine Ed12.

Right, top, centre and bottom: In the latter part of 1929 the Mk IIIM prototype N225 was fitted with a Rolls-Royce F.XII (Kestrel II), with two banks of six cylinders instead of the Lion's three banks of four, and given the now-standard curvaceous fin and a rudder with an aerodynamic balance area inset into the fin trailing edge. The rearmost of the two high-set footholes on the port side of the fuselage was brought forward, and a further low foothole was added to ease access to the rear cockpit. The upper two photographs were taken during trials conducted by the MAEE at Felixstowe.

AUTHOR'S COLLECTION

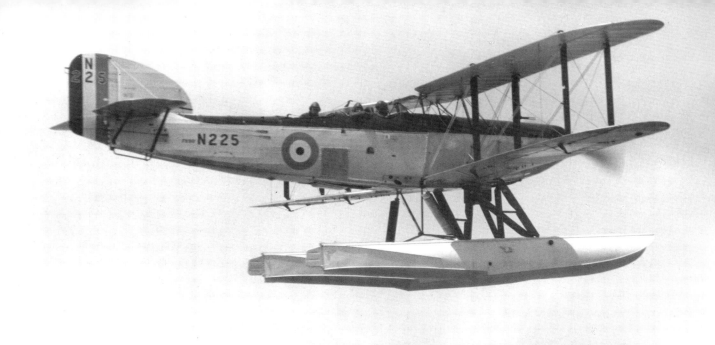

In 1936 the Air Ministry required information on the Junkers Jumo 205C compression ignition (diesel) engine. The engine had failed to pass the Air Ministry type test on two occasions, and it was desired to ascertain its reliability in normal service. Information was also sought regarding its general handling and flight characteristics. The aeroplane chosen to be modified for this task was Fairey IIIF Mk IVB K1726, which had previously served with No 8 Squadron RAF in the Middle East. It went to the RAE on 28 December 1936, and the tests continued until late 1939, being terminated by the outbreak of war and the Engine Executive Committee's decision to cease active work on compression ignition engines. In all, three different Jumos were installed in K1726, one of which was reinstalled a second time after rebuild, and a total of 290¾ hours of flying time was logged. Although no external report was issued in 1939, interest in the engine was revived in the early 1940s, partly owing to the German use of an exhaust turbo-supercharged version of the Jumo 205C in the high-altitude Junkers Ju 86K reconnaissance bomber, and a report was then issued by the RAE in May 1943.

Above: A flying view of the Kestrel-engined Mk IIIM prototype N225.
Below: Fairey IIIF J9154 made its first flight under the power of an Armstrong Siddeley Jaguar VI air-cooled radial on 17 April 1929, becoming the prototype for the Fairey Gordon.

Right: Allocated to its maker for trials with installations of various marks of the Rolls-Royce F XII (Kestrel) engine, IIIF Mk IVM J9174 is seen here at RAE Farnborough, where it spent several periods during its life. This photograph is dated 22 June 1929, at which time the aircraft had a 480hp F.XIIA. It had made its first flight with this engine on 5 December 1928.

AUTHOR'S COLLECTION

Most of the flying time was devoted to endurance testing, but fuel consumption tests were also made, the effect of the removal of the exhaust silencers on performance was ascertained, and the aircraft's ceiling was determined. In addition, information was obtained on the relative effectiveness of the standard compressed-air starting system and the Coffman starter fitted as an alternative to all except the first engine installed. During the last sixty-five flying hours K1726 was allocated to various RAF units for Service trials, these tests being terminated by the outbreak of war.

The Jumo 205C was a vertical, six-cylinder, inline, opposed-piston, liquid-cooled engine, operating on the two-stroke cycle. It had a swept volume of 16.62 litres (1,014 cubic inches) and a maximum output of 592bhp at 2,200rpm. The first Jumo installed in K1726 was maker's No 17312 (Air Ministry No 123153), which amassed 100½ hours; the second, maker's No 30882 (No 128215), accumulated 99½ hours in its first installation; the third, maker's No 17383 (No 135694) flew 37 hours; and finally the rebuilt and reinstalled second engine

Below: The Kestrel-engined J9174 during engine silencing tests conducted at the RAE from 1933 to 1936, with an automobile-type engine silencer on each exhaust pipe. The engine had the lowest standard Kestrel gear ratio and drove a three-bladed metal propeller, the pitch of the blades being adjustable on the ground. The aircraft appeared in this form as No 10 in Event 14 of the RAF Display at Hendon on 24 June 1933, the 'Parade and Fly Past of Present and Experimental Types', being described in the programme as a 'Silence Research Aircraft'.

AUTHOR'S COLLECTION

logged another 53¾hr. On the manufacturer's recommendation, during its initial period of flight each engine was flown at a crankshaft speed not exceeding 1,950rpm, with occasional brief bursts of full power to assist in the process of running-in the fire range.

Before the first engine was installed in K1726, measurements of power, brake mean effective pressure, specific consumption and scavenge air pressure were taken at the Napier works, the company having obtained a licence to manufacture Junkers diesel engines. When installed in the airframe it drove a Junkers three-bladed metal propeller that was used throughout the tests. The propeller had individually adjustable blades, and during the first 31 hours of flight testing 'some slight trouble' was encountered as a result of creep, which allowed the pitch to coarsen by 1¼ degrees during this period and caused scuffing of the blade roots. After the indentation marks were removed the blades turned through 0.4 degrees during the next ten hours of flying, but after readjustment no further trouble was experienced.

After 31 hours' flying, the fire rings of Nos 3 and 5 exhaust pistons were exhibiting signs of blow-by, and after 41 hours, following reports of slight engine roughness, the defective pistons were fitted with new rings. At this time it was discovered that the front main bearing of the top crankshaft was badly scored, and that the crankshaft journal was lightly scored. After cleaning up and refitting the existing bearing, five hours of ground running was completed satisfactorily, the engine speed being increased gradually from 600rpm to 1,830rpm. Flight tests then resumed.

After 71 hours the defective bearing seized as the engine was shut down after flight and, upon examination, the centre portion of both halves of the bearing was found to be badly torn. Moreover, the head of the dowel engaging in the slot milled in the bearing housing had been bearing against the face of the slot,

Right and below: Nearly a Seal! Fairey IIIF Mk III seaplane S1325 as a 'Mk VM', powered by a 525hp Armstrong Siddeley Panther IIA fourteen-cylinder two-row radial, with the MAEE at Felixstowe for trials. Notice the externally mounted Vickers gun on the port fuselage flank. The radial engine ruled out the fixed, forward-firing machine-gun installation used in the inline-engined IIIFs.

possibly causing the bearing to bulge inwards and thus accounting for the failure. The damaged journal was repolished and a new bearing fitted.

In the final 29 hours two 'minor troubles' occurred. First there was a marked vibration period at about 1,800rpm, which was overcome by increasing the pressure of the vibration damper oil. Then came a sudden loss of 40rpm in flight, while cruising at 1,900rpm, after 98 hours' flying time. This loss could not be reproduced on the ground, so it was decided to complete the 100-hour schedule. The subsequent strip examination of the engine showed its general condition to

be satisfactory, the only important defect being the failure of the drive to one of the two fuel circulating pumps. The second Jumo was now installed, and flown under light load during the initial twelve hours and under normal operating conditions thereafter. The 100-hour schedule was completed without major trouble.

The fire rings, which were only in fair condition when the engine was installed, improved with running and were in excellent condition at the end of the schedule. There was a slight drop in oil pressure after 63 hours of flying, but after cleaning the pressure filter, which was found to contain a small quantity of aluminium in addition to normal sediment, the pressure returned to normal. At 78 hours the engine developed roughness. The filter was found to be quite clean, and after venting of the fuel system the roughness disappeared.

During the routine inspection following completion of the 100-hour schedule, metal was again found in the pressure filter. As the scavenge filter was free from metal, the engine was removed for an examination of the pressure oil pump, whereupon it was found that the pump housing was badly scored over the region swept by the gear pump teeth. In addition, a length of steel locking wire was found loose in the sump. One main bearing cap was removed for examination, and the bearing was found to be slightly ridged and in unsatisfactory condition. Consequently, tests with this engine were discontinued and it was subsequently returned to Germany to be rebuilt.

The third engine was now installed in K1726, and, following the satisfactory completion of an initial 25-hour period at the RAE, the aircraft was allotted to No 2 Anti Aircraft Co-operation Unit at Lee-on-Solent, which it joined on 31 December 1938. After 37 hours a major failure occurred while K1726 was being flown at the Station, probably owing to seizure of the fire ring on No 1 exhaust piston. This caused the piston to break up, and the connecting rod, which also broke, fractured the crankcase and top cover.

The rebuilt second engine was then reinstalled at Lee-on-Solent, and completed 17 hours there without incident. Subsequent inspection at the RAE revealed aluminium particles embedded in the upper front main bearing, and light scoring on several pistons, apparently due to incomplete removal of swarf from the oil system following the engine's previous failure. The vertical clearance of the fore rings on three exhaust pistons was found to be 'somewhat excessive'.

After the main bearing had been burnished and reassembled, and the oil system thoroughly cleaned, the engine satisfactorily completed two hours of ground running and five of flying at the RAE. The IIIF was then delivered to the RAF School of Aeronautical Engineering at Henlow on 2 June 1939 for continuation of the Service trials. Following another 25 hours of flying the engine was again examined at the RAE. As no further deterioration was evident, K1726 was dispatched to No 142 Squadron at Bicester, a day bomber unit equipped with Fairey Battles, on 5 October 1939. The aircraft was returned to the RAE on 28 November, the rebuilt second engine having flown 53¾ hours since its complete overhaul. Fairey IIIF K1726 was struck off charge on 10 March 1941.

The first Jumo 205C installed in K1726 was equipped for compressed-air starting. It was fitted with an auxiliary starting carburettor arranged to spray a mixture of 50 per cent lubricating oil, 25 per cent fuel oil and 25 per cent ethyl ether into the one induction pipe. While this system was very satisfactory with a warm engine, it was 'decidedly bad' for a start from cold, particularly at low air temperatures. On all subsequent engines, therefore, a Coffman type L.3 starter was fitted, although the compressed-air starting system was retained. The Coffman

Below: In a protracted period of testing at RAE Farnborough, from late December 1936 to late 1939, no fewer than three different Junkers Jumo 205C compression ignition (diesel) engines were tested in Fairey IIIF Mk VB K1726. Undoubtedly the ugliest IIIF of all, it also flew in this form with No 2 Anti-Aircraft Co-operation Unit at Lee-on-Solent, with the RAF School of Aeronautical Engineering at Henlow and with No 142 Squadron at Bicester.

Right: A 520hp Bristol Jupiter VIII nine-cylinder radial engine driving a four-bladed metal propeller gave the nose of J9150, seen here at Northolt, rather less elegant lines. The aircraft was also tested as a seaplane with this engine.

starter proved very successful, starts being obtained from cold at the first attempt on practically every occasion.

Apart from a marked period of vibration when idling at around 760rpm, and a violent shudder when shutting down, the Jumos ran remarkably smoothly and were free from noticeable vibration throughout the speed range. Response to movement of the fuel injection control lever was immediate, but some care was needed to prevent the engine from stopping when the aircraft touched down to land after gliding in with the lever in the slow running position. The absence of any altitude fuel metering control made it necessary progressively to decrease the maximum opening of the injection lever with increase of height, to prevent the injection of excess fuel and the consequent incomplete combustion and emission of black smoke.

It was reported that 'very little maintenance was necessary or even possible'. The fire rings on the upper pistons were examined at each 30-hour inspection, and on such other occasions as were thought advisable, by the removal of the exhaust manifolds and inspection through the ports. The inlet fire rings could be similarly inspected by the removal of plugs in the induction pipes, though such inspection was not normally necessary. Although lubricating oil filters were inspected at intervals for the presence of metal, it was found inadvisable to remove either the fuel oil filter or injection nozzles owing to their extreme fineness and the danger of introducing foreign matter.

The effect of height on the rates of fuel consumption over a range of airspeeds and crankshaft speeds was investigated on the first and third engines with similar results. As might have been expected with such engines, fuel economy was 'exceptional'. Tests were made with and without the RAE-type silencers, and no difference in performance or consumption was detected within experimental limits. However, the fitting of silencers effected a great reduction in exhaust noise, which was otherwise 'objectionably prominent'.

The absolute ceilings of the second and third Jumos in K1726 were 15,400 feet and 15,200 feet, respectively. Take-off and rate of climb were normal, 'taking into account the considerable all-up weight of the aeroplane'.

It was concluded that the Jumo 205C's weak points were the upper front main bearing and the exhaust piston fire rings, both of which were liable to give trouble without warning. Otherwise the engine was 'singularly free from trouble', and required little maintenance. The report stated that the engine's performance rendered it unsuitable for military use, although its exceptional economy would have shown to the advantage on long-range commercial operations.

'Considerable Interest'

British Civil-Registered Fairey IIIFs

IN September 1928 Fairey ordered a IIIF Mk IIIM for company use as a demonstrator, and c/n F1129 was given the civil registration G-AABY. The aircraft, which had a Lion XIA/civil, was assembled and tested at Fairey's aerodrome at Northolt, making its maiden flight on 15 July 1929, after which it was briefly shown off at a Heston Garden Party in connection with the Aero Show at Olympia in London.

On 30 July 1929 pilot Captain Charles McMullin, accompanied by engineer Charles Baker, left Croydon Airport, England, for Greece in G-AABY, to take part in a competition organised by the Greek Government to select new machines for their air forces. Helped by a tailwind, only 90 minutes after leaving Croydon they arrived at Brussels, where the Belgian authorities, including all the principal general officers commanding the Belgian Air Force, inspected the IIIF 'with considerable interest'. Next day they flew to Vienna via Frankfurt, and from there the aircraft went on to Belgrade, Yugoslavia, on 1 August, this leg taking 3 hours 10 minutes. Here, further demonstrations for officials took place. Then another flight of just over three hours took them to Salonika, whence, after refuelling, the aircraft was flown direct to Tatoi Aerodrome, Athens, in 2 hours 15 minutes.

At Tatoi there were several reconnaissance and single-seater military aircraft of different nationalities, all in search of orders, so the IIIF faced stiff competition. Its particular competitors were a French Breguet 19 and a Czech Letov-Smolik (fitted with dummy wooden guns in the rear cockpit). The first few days were devoted to a detailed inspection of the machines by the Greek Military Commission, and the IIIF's construction was 'openly admired on all sides'. Then came the flying demonstrations, embracing a climb, speed run, etc., at various altitudes, designed to compare the performances of the competitors, plus general

Below: Fairey's IIIF Mk IIIM company demonstrator, G-AABY, powered by a Lion XIA/civil, first flew on 15 July 1929. It survived until August 1937, spending the last years of its life in Australia.

demonstration flights carrying Greek army officers. The IIIF attained almost 150mph in a speed contest, which was good in the prevailing conditions, and won a test of speed at 4,000 metres over a 100-kilometre course so easily that the Greeks thought it too good to be true and requested that it be repeated. The demonstrations were completed on 17 August 'with complete success'.

A serious difficulty was posed by the next stage, in which the float chassis had to be fitted for a demonstration of the aircraft's capabilities as a seaplane. Tatoi aerodrome was some twenty-five miles from the naval seaplane station in Phaleron Bay, on the other side of Athens, and the interconnecting roads were 'rather difficult and in some places rough'. A suitable field for a safe landing near Phaleron could not be found, and as the Fairey team was disinclined to risk an accident the aircraft's wings and tailplane were removed with the aid of a crew of Greek sailors, and the machine was towed behind a lorry to the naval base. The

Above: In 1929, after staging across Europe and making demonstration flights en route, G-AABY took part in a competition to select new military aircraft for the Greek air forces. It is seen here in seaplane configuration off the island of Hydra, with the summer palace of the Greek President in the background.

Left: In October and November 1934 G-AABY was flown in the MacRobertson Trophy Race from England to Australia by Flying Officer C. G. Davies and Lieutenant-Commander C. N. Hill.

Left: The starting point for the MacRoberston Race was Mildenhall, where G-AABY is seen here being prepared in October 1934. The aircraft was named *Time and Chance*, but the name is not visible in any of the accompanying pictures.

AUTHOR'S COLLECTION

day-long trip was rather hair-raising, as some very steep corners, with sheer drops in many places, had to be negotiated, and overhanging trees threatened to damage the upper wing centre section.

Three days were then spent reassembling G-AABY and fitting the float chassis, which had been shipped to Phaleron Bay in advance. The aircraft flew as a seaplane on 24 August, and the next few days were spent demonstrating the configuration to the Greek Naval Department and carrying more officers and officials on exhibition flights. This done, the problem arose of getting the aircraft back to Tatoi in landplane form. Fortunately another long tow along the difficult roads was avoided, as a piece of waste ground not more than 100 yards long was found just behind an aircraft factory near the seaplane base. After being held back by mechanics until McMullin had got the throttle wide open and given the release signal, the duly lightened IIIF took off from the site without difficulty. This impressed the massed watching naval base personnel, who had doubted whether it

Below: With Davies in the cockpit and Hill on the right of the picture, G-AABY undergoes checks at Mildenhall on 18 October 1934. They were in vain: the aircraft had to be retired from the race and did not arrive in Melbourne until 23 November, well after the specified time limit.

217

Above and left: Fairey IIIF G-AASK, fitted with a Jaguar VIC geared radial, was modified for the Air Survey Company late in 1929 and was one of two flown to undertake aerial survey work in the Sudan .

could get off from so small an area and thought the Englishmen crazy to attempt it. Thus, while it had taken about twelve arduous hours to get from Tatoi to Phaleron, the return journey took a mere ten minutes.

Having completed his demonstrations, McMullin flew G-AABY back to Croydon via Uskub (Skopje), Belgrade, Vienna, Nuremberg and Cologne, completing the trip in 14 hours 35 minutes. In Yugoslavia he gave a demonstration at Novi Said military aerodrome, and then flew Prince Paul (the future King Paul of the Hellenes) to England to see the Schneider Trophy contest. On return he reported: 'Throughout the trip we had not the slightest trouble with either the aircraft or the Napier Lion XI engine, and although it entailed a lot of hard work, Baker and myself enjoyed ourselves heartily'.

Later G-AABY was fitted with an Armstrong Siddeley Panther IIA radial, delivered to East India Docks by Lep Transport on 26 March 1931, and shipped out to Arnhold & Co of Shanghai for demonstrations, but it crashed on its first attempted take-off in April and suffered damage that necessitated its return to England for repairs, these being carried out at RAF North Weald, Essex, in 1934.

At this time the aircraft was entered in the handicap section of the October 1934 MacRobertson Trophy Race from England to Australia. Piloted by Flying Officer C. G. Davies, and with Lieutenant Commander C. N. Hill as navigator, it flew as No 15 and was named *Time and Chance*. As a result of delays en route, notably with aileron problems at Nicosia, Cyprus, the aircraft was retired from the race and did not reach Melbourne, the ultimate destination, until 23 November, well after the time limit set for completion of the flight.

In Australia Davies flew G-AABY on charter work for Austral Air Services of Queensland. On 13 March 1935 it was given the Australian registration VH-UTT, and on the 20th it was registered to Major E. G. Clark, trading as Austral Air Services. On 10 April it was sold to long-distance flyer Ray Parer of Wau, New Guinea. On 12 March 1936 its Certificate of Registration lapsed and it was struck off the register, but its C of R was renewed on 25 August the same year. When the C of R lapsed again a year later, on 24 August 1937, VH-UTT was broken up and struck off the register.

Two Jaguar-engined IIIFs, G-AASK (F1272, Jaguar VIC/geared) and G-AATT (F1315, Jaguar VI), were specially modified late in 1929 to work with Air Survey Ltd in the Sudan, the company having recently become a Fairey subsidiary. The first was delivered to Air Survey at Croydon on 1 January 1930, the other following on 6 February that year. After leaving for Juba on 23 January 1930, G-AASK remained in service until the end of 1934. The working life of its sister aircraft, G-AATT, which left Britain on 22 February 1930, was terminated when it was destroyed in a crash that October.

Left and below: G-AATT, which was powered by an Armstrong Siddeley Jaguar VI air-cooled radial engine, was the second of the two IIIFs operated by the Air Survey Company, a Fairey subsidiary. This aircraft was the shorter-lived of the pair: it was destroyed in a crash in October 1930, having been in commission for some eight months only.

219

Spreading Its Wings

The Fairey IIIF in Foreign Service

I N the late 1920s Argentina began to build the *Flota de Mar*, a powerful naval fleet to defend the country's 2,500-mile coastline and vital sea lanes. Ship-borne spotter aircraft were required to enable fleet commanders to see over the horizon, and in 1927 the *Ministerio de Marina* began to seek out a suitable reconnaissance machine for its naval air arm, the *Servicio de Aviación Naval*. On 30 May 1928 the Argentine government signed a contract with Fairey Aviation Company for six Fairey IIIF Mk IIIM (Special) seaplanes, including spares, for £43,580. These aircraft were to operate from the battleship *Rivadavia* in both seaplane and landplane configuration.

In an endeavour to support the nation's aircraft industry, the Argentine government obtained a licence for the Fabrica Militar de Aviones in Provincia de Cordoba to build the French 450hp Lorraine Dietrich Ed12 twelve-cylinder, broad-arrow, liquid-cooled engine, and stipulated that this engine was to be used in all the new aircraft types then being acquired, the Supermarine Southampton, Dewoitine D.21 and Fairey IIIF. Unfortunately the Ed12 was insufficiently powerful for these aircraft, and this misjudged attempt to standardise on one engine type proved to be a costly mistake.

Fairey began production of the Argentine IIIFs almost at once at its Hayes factory, under Works Production Order No 1370. The machines had constructor's numbers F1122 to F1127 and were allotted the Argentine Navy *escuadrilla* (squadron) codes AP-1 to AP-6, respectively. Their Lorraine engines had helmeted cylinder banks. As it was also planned to use the IIIFs for survey work, they were fitted out to carry a Williamson Eagle Mk III camera in fuselage Bay 6, where the

Left and opposite, top and bottom: Views of first of the six Lorraine Dietrich Ed12-engined IIIF Mk IIIM (Specials) for Argentina, AP-1, in landplane configuration shortly after completion. The Argentine government's choice of an insufficiently powerful engine proved to be a costly mistake.

starboard portion of the floor was made removable to permit camera operation. For communications, a Marconi AD-6H wireless telegraph and telephone were provided, the transmitter and receiver being housed in Bay 5. When they were not in use they could be stowed along the starboard side of the fuselage, and could be swung into position diagonally across the fuselage to be operated by the observer. For electrical power a 1,200-volt wind-driven generator on the starboard side of the fuselage was swung out into the slipstream. The 300-foot aerial was wound out from a reel on the starboard side of Bay 4. The armament followed the pattern of the RAF machines.

The fabric-covered areas of the Argentine IIIFs were finished in silver, aluminium-pigmented dope, and the fuselage top-decking from immediately behind the engine to the tailplane was painted in anti-glare matt black. The engine cowlings and light-alloy panels were given an anodised finish, and the 21 foot 9 inch-long duralumin floats were coated with gloss white yacht enamel. The *escuadrilla* codes were applied to the rear fuselage sides, and the Argentine national insignia, of light blue and white horizontal bands with a yellow sun symbol on the central white band, was carried on the rudders. Each aircraft's code was painted in large letters on the upper wing, with anchor symbols towards each wingtip. The first machine, AP-1, was complete by early October 1928, and made its maiden flight as a landplane, in the hands of test pilot Captain Norman Macmillan, on 31 October. Several test flights followed, the machine making its final acceptance flight on 12 November.

Left: Starboard elevation of AP-1, the first IIIF Mk IIIM (Special) for Argentina.

Three days earlier Macmillan had flown AP-2 and AP-3, and the latter aircraft was then delivered to the company's Hamble site for the fitment of Type FE 18 floats in readiness for sea trials. Macmillan conducted the acceptance tests for the Lorraine-engined seaplane at Hamble, off Southampton Water, on 14 November. Endurance, climb, speed and water handling were tested with the Hamble works manager and the senior Argentine naval officer on board as observers.

Macmillan made the first flights of the last three machines, AP-4, AP-5 and AP-6, on 19 November, and the flight test programme was completed on the 23rd. With the exception of some of AP-1's early flights, a representative of the *Comisión Naval Argentina* was carried on all test flights. This duty was shared by delegation leader *Capitán de Navío* Marcos A. Zar, *Jefe del Servicio de Aviación Naval*; *Teniente de Fragata* Gregorio Portillo; and Cabo Juarez. Fairey Works Production Order No 1370 was finally closed on 14 December 1928.

The six aircraft were crated for shipment and left Liverpool docks on 20 January 1929, destined for Puerto Belgrano, Bahía Blanca, Provincia de Buenos Aires. According to the manufacturer's Works Inspection Records, a seventh airframe, c/n F1128, was also included as part of an undisclosed number of spare airframe components which might have comprised a complete disassembled airframe or a collection of major spares.

Fairey engineering representatives assisted in reassembling the aircraft at Puerto Belgrano. Once the aircraft had been test-flown and the requisite customer satisfaction certificates had been signed, they were assigned to the *Escuadrilla de Patrulla y Propósitos Generales* (Patrol and General Duties Squadron) at *Base de Aviatión* Puerto Belgrano, part of the *Base Naval* Puerto Belgrano naval complex at Bahía Blanca.

By the autumn of 1929 *Rivadavia* had been modified to enable it to operate aircraft, mainly by the installation of a crane for aircraft deployment and recovery. On 2 October IIIF AP-2 took part in very promising trials at BN Puerto Belgrano.

From 7 to 13 November AP-1, AP-3 and AP-5 flown, respectively, by *Teniente de Fragata* Evaristo Velo, *Sub-Oficial* Arturo Feilberg and *Alferez de Navío* Juan Carlos Mason, made a series of survey flights over Caleta Valdez, Provincia de Chubut, supported by Keystone K 24A Pelican HE-16. In January 1930 AP-1 and AP-2, flown by *Teniente de Fragata* Alberto Sautu Riestra and *Sub-Oficial* Arturo Feilberg, respectively, carried out aerial survey photography flights over the Río Negro and Río Limay rivers, being deployed to Bariloche, Provincia de Río Negro for the purpose.

On 2 February 1931 the pilot of AP-3 wrecked the aircraft's undercarriage, engine and wings when he landed on an 'unsuitable field' at Puerto Romero

This page (and overleaf): A sequence of photographs taken as the second of Argentina's Fairey IIIFs, AP-2, in seaplane form, taxies up to the battleship *Rivadavia* and is hoisted on board during trials at Puerto Belgrano naval base on 2 October 1929. It transpired that water-based operations were not a practical proposition with the French engines.

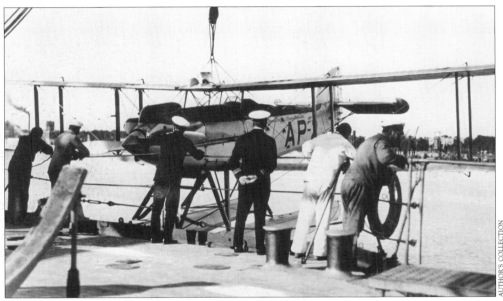

AUTHOR'S COLLECTION

AUTHOR'S COLLECTION

AUTHOR'S COLLECTION

Left: The Argentine IIIF AP-3 undergoes pre-delivery waterborne trials on the Hamble River, November 1928.

AUTHOR'S COLLECTION

Chico, Provincia de Rio Negro, while on a co-operation flight with the *Comisión Hidrográfica de Puerto Belgrano*. The three crew escaped injury and the IIIF was repaired.

Although they had initially been assigned to patrol duties, in 1931 the IIIFs were reassigned to reconnaissance work and joined the newly formed *Escuadrilla de Reconocimiento de la Flota de Mar* (Fleet Reconnaissance Squadron). For this rôle they were given the codes R-51 to R-56, the first in a new series for observation and reconnaissance aircraft. The IIIFs supported the *Flota de Mar* during its

Below: Fairey IIIFs AP-3, AP-5 and AP-1 in service in Argentina.
Bottom: Fairey IIIFs AP-1 and AP-2 moored on the River Limay in Provincia de Rio Negro, possibly in January 1930.

ARCHIVO GENERAL DE LA ARMADA ARGENTINA

COURTESY JUAN CARLOS CICALESI

operations from BA Puerto Belgrano. The first of the type to be lost was R-52, which flew into thick fog while making a cross-country flight from Aeródromo de Campo Sarimento on 16 July 1931 and crashed in a field near Villa Arias, Provincia de Buenos Aires. The three crew members were injured. The aircraft, which had amassed a total flying time of 182 hours 40 minutes, was written off. Then R-53 (ex-AP-3) survived an emergency landing at Campo Sarimento on 17 October.

Later in 1931 R-53, R-54, R-55 and R-56 were assigned to the new *Escuadrilla de Bombardeo Liviano y Exploración* (Light Bombing and Exploration Squadron) at Estación Aeronaval Punta Indio, Verónica, Provincia de Buenos Aires. The other machine, R-51, remained at Puerto Belgrano.

On 17 November 1931 the engine of R-56 failed as it took off from Aerodromo de Concordia, Provincia de Entre Rios, for a test flight, and the aircraft overturned on landing. Its pilot was unhurt and the machine was repaired.

The following year all five IIIFs were reassigned yet again, this time to *Escuadrilla Aeronaval de Reconocimiento de la Escuadra Aeronaval* (Naval Air Fleet Reconnaissance Squadron) No 2. On 22 March 1932 R-54 suffered an engine failure after take-off from Punta Indio, but was returned to service.

While the aircraft were still performing valuable service, their Ed 12 engines had proved insufficiently powerful for water-based operations. Moreover, the indigenous licensed engine manufacturer was seldom able to supply replacement components because the raw materials failed to arrive from France. Consequently, orders ceased to be placed with the Argentine company, the *Aviación Naval* dealing directly with Société Commerciale Lorraine in 1932. Things came to a head when the French company ceased production of the Ed 12 and the orders for spares became special custom requests. This resulted in extended delivery times and a steep rise in prices, a single cylinder block, for example, increasing from US $350 in 1928 to US $1,200 six years later. From 1930 to 1934 a phenomenal US $800,000 was spent on Lorraine engine spares. As a result the *Aviación Naval* could barely keep its Ed 12s serviceable, though the IIIF's

Top, left and right: The wreckage of R-52, the first Argentine IIIF to be written off, after it flew into thick fog and crashed near Villa Arias, Provincia de Buenos Aires, on 16 July 1931.
Above, left: The wings, undercarriage and engine of AP-3 were wrecked when its pilot landed on an unsuitable field at Puerto Romero Chico, Provincia de Rio Negro, on 2 February 1931, but the crew were unharmed and the aircraft was repaired.
Above, right: The upper-wing markings of Argentine IIIFs are clearly depicted in this shot of R-53 after its emergency landing at Campo Sarimento on 17 October 1931.

Peurto Belgrano. Temporarily assigned to training school *Escuadra Aérea No 1*, they were used to train pilots in photography, gunnery and bombing techniques. The next IIIF to be lost was R-55, which, after only four months in service in its rejuvenated form, was struck off charge on 10 August 1935 after an emergency landing at Campo Sarimento airfield while flying circuits. Its pilot was unhurt.

In November 1935, on behalf of *Parques Nacionales*, Argentina's national parks organisation, the IIIFs R-51 and R-53, flown by *Teniente* Exequiel del Rivero and *Teniente* Angel Vaccari, respectively, along with Seal R-54 piloted by *Teniente* Pedro P. Rivero, carried out a series of survey flights over the Río Colorado, Río Neuquen and Río Limay rivers and several Andean lakes. Support was provided by Fokker Universal T-201. On 28 August 1936 R-51 suffered an engine failure after take-off from Campo Sarimento, stalled and crashed. The three crewmen were injured, but the aircraft was repaired.

In 1937 the IIIFs and the Seal joined four Corsairs to take up an observation rôle in support of the *Escuadra de Ríos*, responsible for patrolling the nation's rivers. The newly formed unit became *Escuadrilla de Observación de la Escuadra Aeronaval No 3*, based at EA Punta Indio. In their new rôle the IIIFs were re-coded 3-O-1, 3-O-2 and 3-O-4, the Seal becoming 3-O-3. (The '3' denoted the unit and the 'O' stood for *Observación*.) On 26 August 1940 3-O-1 was damaged when it swung after landing at Punta India, and on 17 December that year its engine failed near General Lavalle, Buenos Aires, but its crew was unhurt.

In 1939 the IIIFs and the Seal were relegated to second-line duties at EA Punta Indio. Of the IIIFs, 3-O-1 and 3-O-2 were struck off charge in 1941, and 3-O-4 was struck off in 1942, along with the Seal.

* * *

In early 1928 the New Zealand Government ordered two Mk IIIMs (Lion XIA), 'one for Wigram aerodrome (landplane) and one for the Air Force Base at Hobsonville (seaplane)'. However, it seems that the idea of retaining one at Wigram was abandoned, and both were based at Hobsonville, being flown south as required. The initial plan was to establish a Coastal Reconnaissance Flight and a Bomber Reconnaissance Flight, of which the two IIIFs were to form the nucleii, but this did not come to pass.

The two aircraft, c/ns F1133 and F1134, which bore these identities as their military New Zealand Permanent Air Force (NZPAF) serials (but are alleged to have later become NZ631 and NZ632), were shipped in the *Port Melbourne* in June 1929, arriving at Auckland on 20 September. Assembled in the hangar at Hobsonville, they were both fitted out as landplanes at first, pending the availability of

Opposite page, top: Seal R-54 and IIIFs R-51 and R-53, which carried out a series of survey flights for Argentina's national parks organisation in November 1935.
Opposite page, centre: A Fairey Seal (right) and IIIF (left), both Panther-powered, photographed in landplane configuration on 6 September 1935. Notice the externally mounted Vickers E gun on the port fuselage sides, necessitated by this engine's greater frontal area and its Townend exhaust collector ring. The twin-engine monoplane visible behind the IIIF is the *Armada Argentina*'s one and only Douglas Dolphin amphibian.
Opposite page, bottom: Fairey IIIF R-53 runs up its Panther engine in preparation for a flight.

Left: The first of the two IIIF Mk IIIMs originally acquired by the Royal New Zealand Permanent Air Force was c/n F1133, which is seen here at Hobsonville, complete with underwing auxiliary fuel tanks, shortly after assembly.

Left: The bedraggled remains of F1134 at Hobsonville Wharf after its recovery on 30 October 1930 following its high-speed ditching on the previous day. The accident was attributed to an error of judgement by its pilot, Flight Lieutenant S. Wallingford, who was flying low over the water when the floats touched the surface and dug in, causing the aircraft to overturn.

RNZAF MUSEUM RESEARCH COLLECTION

facilities enabling them to be used as seaplanes. In December 1929 F1133 made its first flight from the base, and it was the largest aircraft to attend the Auckland Aero Club Pageant at Mangere on 12 April 1930.

New Zealand's Public Works Department then planned an aerial survey of the Central Irrigation Scheme in the Maniototo district of Central Otago, and Flight Lieutenant M. W. Buckley went from Wigram to Auckland to collect F1134 for the task, flying it south on 1 May 1930 and covering the 555 miles in a flying time of 4 hours 55 minutes. For the survey, Buckley flew the IIIF as a landplane from Ranfurly, carrying a photographer and his equipment. Four 'photographic' days (when conditions were ideal) were spent covering some 300 square miles of hill country, though the task was not completed. On 10 May Buckley and his passenger took aerial photographs of Christchurch from 8,000 feet. He flew F1134 back to Hobsonville on 11 June, leaving Wigram at 9.50 a.m. and arriving at his destination at 1.30 p.m. thanks to a strong southerly gale of 35mph, which gave the IIIF a remarkable ground speed of 145mph and an airspeed of about 110mph.

The aircraft was returned to Hobsonville before the work was finished so that both IIIFs could take part in the combined naval and aerial manœuvres in the Hauraki Gulf during June. The aircraft carried out drogue-towing, torpedo-spotting and observation of fire, the exercises ending on 20 June. Thus was initiated co-operation in torpedo, gunnery and anti-aircraft exercises with the New Zealand Division of the Royal Navy, which lasted until 1936, when the Division was able to supply its own aircraft in the form of Supermarine Walruses.

The survey was then resumed, F1134 being flown back to Wigram on 28 June by Squadron Leader L. M. Isitt, Hobsonville's CO. Upon completion of the survey it was returned to Hobsonville and then restored to floatplane configuration on 18 July.

On 2 October 1930 Flight Lieutenant Buckley took two civilian passengers, Dr Viloet Bergers of New York and Polish journalist Mr Czerniewski, for a flight over and around Mount Cook at an altitude of 16,000 feet, probably in F1133, Dr Bergers being the first woman in the world to make the trip.

On 29 October 1930 Flight Lieutenant S. Wallingford, carrying Corporal H. Smith and Aircraft Apprentice A. G. Andrews as passengers in F1134, flew in

Right: New Zealand's Mk IIIB, S.1805, taxying at speed. This aircraft was still performing useful work in 1939.

RNZAF MUSEUM RESEARCH COLLECTION

salute over a departing flotilla of the East Indies Squadron of the Royal Netherlands Navy at 11.15 a.m., as it left Auckland at the end of a goodwill visit. Towards midday Wallingford decided to make a high-speed test flight at low level over a known course about a mile and a half off the city side of Hobsonville, in the upper harbour off Birkdale. He brought the IIIF low over the water, attaining 146mph, but in slowing down shortly afterwards its floats touched the water at about 126mph and dug in. The seaplane overturned, and its three occupants were thrown out underwater as the machine virtually disintegrated. Squadron Leader Isitt, who had been flying behind the IIIF in a Saunders-Roe Cutty Sark flying boat, alighted and picked up the three men, none of whom was injured. All had been wearing kapok lifejackets, and none had been strapped in, to which they attributed their rapid rise to the surface. Although the subsequent Court of Inquiry attributed the accident to an error of judgement by the pilot, it concluded that he had conducted the speed trials within the scope of his duty, and that no blame should be attached to him or to any other person.

Above: The replacement for F1134 was Mk IIIB S1805, c/n F1542, which was sold to the NZPAF on 4 October 1933, some three years after F1134's loss. This machine had the later triple exhaust pipe system.

RNZAF MUSEUM RESEARCH COLLECTION

All the light components of F1134 were badly smashed, and it sank in about 60 feet of water. The site was marked, and salvage began on 30 October. The aircraft was stuck inverted in the mud, its propeller was missing and its forward fuselage was twisted to the right at an acute angle. It was described as a jumbled heap of frame and fabric. After attempting to raise the aircraft using a steel cable attached to the fuselage, in the end both the salvage barge and the aircraft were towed to Hobsonville Wharf, where a crane with a lifting capacity of three tons lifted it out of the water. The wreckage was then inspected in the hangar. Although the annual report for 31 May 1931 stated that F1134 had been returned to Fairey for reconditioning, it appears that this was not so, as the wreckage remained at Hobsonville for several years.

Thus F1133 was left to perform the mercy flights, naval co-operation duties and general-purpose flying on its own. On 3 December 1930, during naval exercises with HMS *Dunedin* in the Hauraki Gulf, it was diverted from its drogue-towing and spotting duties to carry a doctor from Auckland to Great Barrier Island to attend an injured seaman. On 9 December F1133 made a 5½-hour staged flight from Hobsonville to Wigram, the Director of Air Services and Wigram's CO maintaining radio contact with the IIIF throughout the flight.

During late 1931 and early 1933 F1133 carried out five distinct series of naval co-operation exercises 'of considerable value' with the cruiser HMS *Diomede*. They included searching, height-finding, sleeve-target practice, observation of shot and camera-gun practice. This work continued in 1932–33, the IIIF logging 67 flying hours throughout the year on these naval co-operation duties, which also included search and interception and low-flying attack practices.

In the 1931/1932 annual report it had been stated that 'If naval co-operation is to continue on the same scale an additional Fairey IIIF is essential', and S1805 (c/n F1542), a Mk IIIB from an 87-aircraft batch of IIIF Mk IIIs for the RAF, was recorded as being sold to the NZPAF on 4 October 1933, However, the New Zealand annual report on the air services stated that it was ordered in November 1932, and it arrived at Auckland aboard the *Northumberland* on 23 May 1933! (It is alleged to have become NZ633.) Within a fortnight of its arrival it had been assembled at Hobsonville. Although this aircraft was stressed for catapulting from capital ships, it is not known whether it was supplied with catapult equipment, and it was never catapulted while in NZPAF service.

When the Australian cruisers *Canberra* and *Australia* exercised in northern New Zealand waters with *Diomede* and *Dunedin* between 23 and 31 August 1933, the

Above: The surviving NZPAF IIIF Mk IIIM, F1133, in front of a line-up of civil and military de Havilland D.H.60 Moths at Hobsonville Aerodrome, *circa* 1934. The nearest Moth is ZK-AAR *Falcon*, and immediately behind it are 871 and 870 in NZPAF markings.

Right: A parting shot from an unusual angle of an NZPAF Fairey IIIF as its taxies away at speed.

235

Supermarine Seagulls borne by the Australian vessels carried out naval co-operation with the two IIIFs, which were operated as seaplanes. Towards the end of 1933 F1133 underwent a complete overhaul and reconditioning at Hobsonville.

The IIIF's carrying capacity was demonstrated on 19 January 1934, when S1805 flew to Dunedin via Wigram to deliver 100 pounds of supplies to Commander Richard Byrd's Antarctic Expedition. As well as carrying an observer, the aircraft, in landplane configuration, carried fifty blankets, thirty pairs of boots and a quantity of jackets, vests and moleskin coats.

During February and April 1934 the normal co-operation duties with the Navy were carried out. On 27 February the NZPAF became the RNZAF; the only Service aircraft based at Hobsonville were the two IIIFs. In 1934 and 1935 the aircraft took part in air mail flights. On 3 February 1935 a IIIF took part in a dramatic rescue of a woman swimmer who had been swept out to sea off Karekare Beach, Auckland. On 17 June 1935 S1805, fully loaded with heavy sleeve targets and equipment, was unable to take off from Waitemata Harbour in conditions of no wind and low tide.

The IIIFs were still requested to attend flying club pageants in 1936 and 1937, and several ambulance flights were made in the late 1930s. By this time the provision of shipborne aircraft on the cruisers of the New Zealand Station considerably reduced the demand for the IIIFs for co-operation work. However, as late as March 1939 S1805 was based at Hastings on army co-operation exercises in company with a Walrus from HMS *Achilles*. The Napier area's 22nd Anti-Aircraft Battery fired short shell bursts at the IIIF.

Both of the IIIFs were officially grounded in 1941, though their flying careers had probably ended some time earlier. They finished their lives as instructional airframes at Hobsonville Technical Training Centre, having outlasted many of their intended successors (F1133 became INST 2, and S1805 became INST 18). They are believed to have been broken up towards the end of World War II.

* * *

As a result of the European demonstration flights described earlier, in October 1930 the Greek Government initially ordered a single IIIF Mk I. This was followed on 23 July 1931 by the delivery of ten Mk IIIBs with Lion XIA engines, c/ns F1479–1488, as seaplanes for the nation's naval air service. Finished in aluminium dope and natural metal, with black fuselage top-decking, they went to Hamble on 10, 11, 12, 13, 16, 16, 18, 19, 21 and 24 February, respectively, carried the serials N1 to N12 and had national insignia on the fuselage, wings and tail. *Flight* reported in its issue for 20 March, 1931, that a batch of six IIIFs for Greece 'were put through their tests at Fairey's Hamble seaplane station last week before Captain Phocas, Greek Naval Attaché, and Lieut-Comm Averoff, of the Greek Navy'. These aircraft were fitted with floats of a new type. In addition to the normal transverse step they had a fore-and-aft step along each chine from the bow to the transverse step—in other words, the 'vee' bottom did not extend right to the chine, but joined a horizontal surface some 6 inches wide, which extended inboard from the chine. *Flight* reported: 'The float shape, although of such simple lines that no panel beating is required, has a marked influence on the clean running, the fore and aft steps deflecting the water and preventing the spray from rising to any great height. In alighting, the sharp vee bottom of the aft portion of the floats cut in with scarcely any spray, and the machines land remarkably cleanly.' In 1935–36, S1189 (F913), S1377 (F1239), S1786 and S1817 were also sold to Greece. In October 1940 No 11 Navy Co-operation Squadron had nine operational IIIFs.

Left: The handing-over of six Fairey IIIF Mk IIIBs to the Greek Government took place at Hamble, Southampton, on 12 March 1931. Here Fairey director Mr Hazell speaks into the microphone shielded by his coat. Captain Phocas, the Greek Naval Attaché, is standing immediately next to him.

Left and below: Two of a series of press photographs taken on the occasion of the handing over of six IIIFs to the Greek Government on 12 March 1931.

The Irish Army Air Corps had Mk II S1262 (c/n F968), delivered on 10 March 1928. The aircraft crashed at 31 Terenure Road, on the outskirts of Dublin, at 3.15 p.m. on 10 September 1934, reportedly during a trial flight. Two of the occupants were killed and one survived. Two further IIIFs are said to have been ordered but were cancelled. One source quotes the serials J9053 and J9054—IIIFs Mk IVC (GP) from a fifteen-aircraft batch for the RAF—which were c/ns F969 and F970 (following on directly from S1262 in the manufacturer's c/n series), but the RAF serial records make no mention of these aircraft ever being destined for Ireland. Another source identifies them as Mk IIIMs c/ns F1135 & F1136, with no previous RAF or FAA serials.

* * *

A number of other nations took delivery of Fairey IIIFs. The Royal Canadian Air Force had IIIF Mk IV GP J9172 (F1038) on loan. Taken on strength on 7 October 1929, it underwent cold-weather trials as a floatplane at Victoria Beach. It was struck off charge on 16 September 1930 and returned to Britain, where it was with the Home Aircraft Depot on 25 November. It went to No 207

Below: Another of the press photographs taken on 12 March 1931. The occasion saw one of the Greek seaplanes taxiing out and making a demonstration flight over the others.

AUTHOR'S COLLECTION

Left: Taken from a thirteen-aircraft batch for the Fleet Air Arm, the Irish Army Air Corps' Fairey IIIF Mk II, S1262, was delivered on 10 March 1928. It met its end in a fatal crash on the outskirts of Dublin on 10 September 1934.

Squadron on 31 November 1931, then returned to HAD on 16 September 1932 and was overhauled and converted to a Gordon.

Four Lion V-engined Mk Is (F976–979) and a single Mk IIIB (F1514) were bought for the Chilean Navy. These aircraft, which had rounded fins but rudders that were rather squarer than the norm, became Nos 23–26 in Chilean service. A

Right: The second of the four Lion V-engined IIIF Mk Is built for the Chilean Navy, No 24 (c/n F977), displays the original vertical tail surfaces adopted for these export aircraft—generally similar to those of the later-standard IIIF but featuring a more angular rudder (as shown in close-up in the photograph overleaf).
Below: The third Chilean IIIF, No 25, makes a low fly-past for the photographer during the manufacturer's pre-delivery tests.

Right: The tail unit of a IIIF Mk I destined for Chile, showing the balanced rudder and elevator. The rudder is of slightly greater area than those of other IIIFs and has a different outline. Notice the flotation bags inside the rear fuselage.

Mk IIIB seaplane for the Chilean Air Mission was delivered to Fairey's Hamble base in January 1931. In addition, Mk IIIs F1514, F2116 and F2117 ('3') were delivered in 1935. These had fins and rudders of the type fitted to the Fairey Gordon and Seal, giving the aircraft a somewhat hybrid appearance.

Arcos Ltd, a predecessor of Aviaexport, took delivery of Lion XIA-engined Mk IVM/A c/n F1478 for Russia on 30 September 1930, but searches in Russian archives have failed to reveal any records of this aircraft arriving at its supposed ultimate destination. Egypt bought J9651 in April 1939. Finally, an order for IIIFs was proposed for the Latvian Air Force's Naval Air Division but was not taken up.

Below: One of the three later IIIF Mk IIIs supplied to Chile, c/n F2117/'3', showing its later exhaust system and Gordon/ Seal type fin and rudder.

Colours and Markings

A Selection of Fairey IIIF Paint Schemes

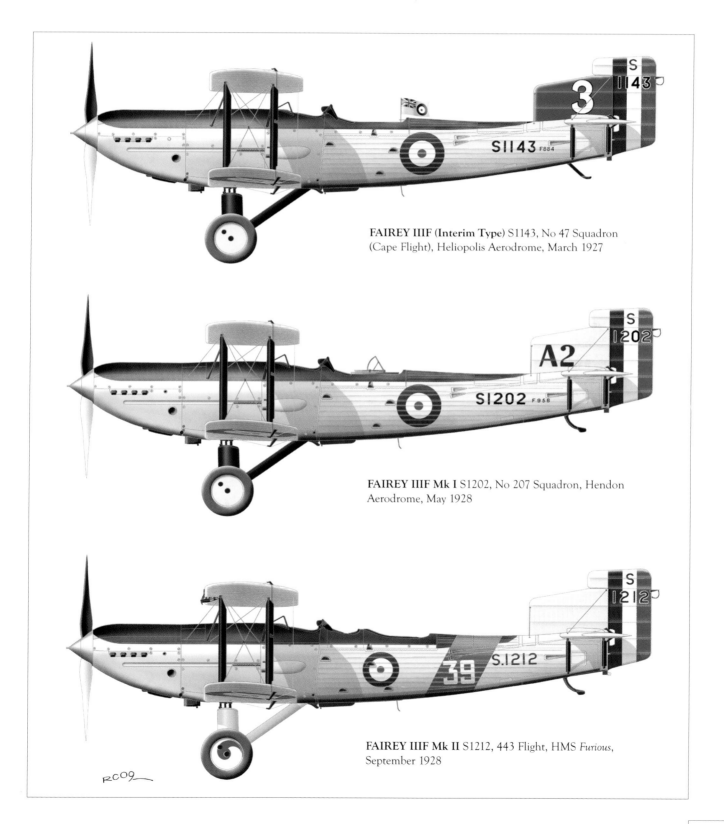

FAIREY IIIF (Interim Type) S1143, No 47 Squadron
(Cape Flight), Heliopolis Aerodrome, March 1927

FAIREY IIIF Mk I S1202, No 207 Squadron, Hendon
Aerodrome, May 1928

FAIREY IIIF Mk II S1212, 443 Flight, HMS *Furious*,
September 1928

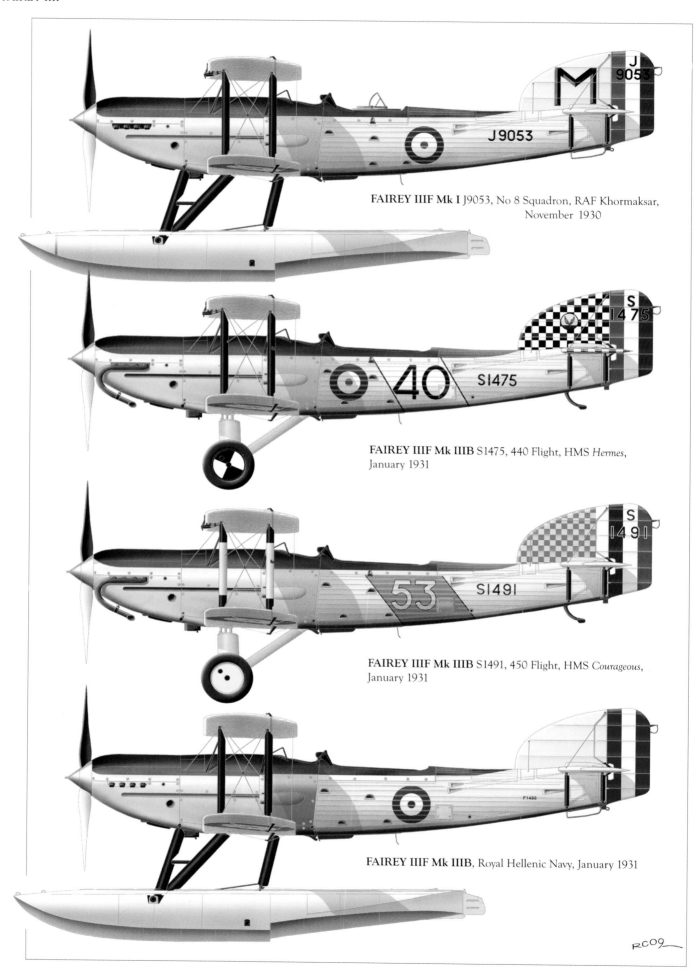

FAIREY IIIF Mk I J9053, No 8 Squadron, RAF Khormaksar, November 1930

FAIREY IIIF Mk IIIB S1475, 440 Flight, HMS *Hermes*, January 1931

FAIREY IIIF Mk IIIB S1491, 450 Flight, HMS *Courageous*, January 1931

FAIREY IIIF Mk IIIB, Royal Hellenic Navy, January 1931

RC09

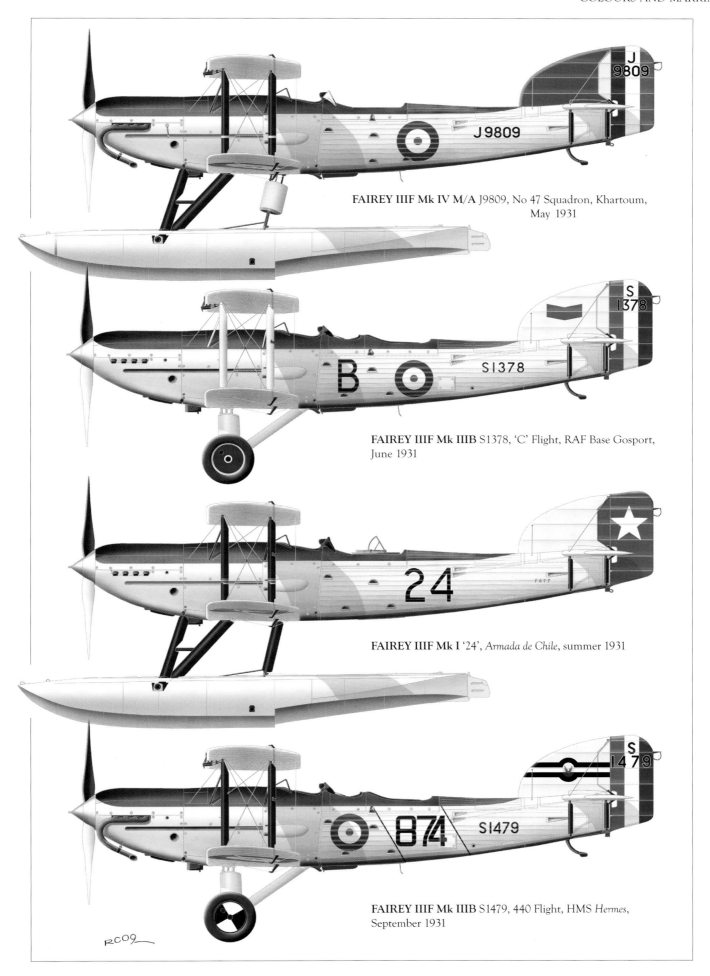

FAIREY IIIF Mk IV M/A J9809, No 47 Squadron, Khartoum, May 1931

FAIREY IIIF Mk IIIB S1378, 'C' Flight, RAF Base Gosport, June 1931

FAIREY IIIF Mk I '24', *Armada de Chile*, summer 1931

FAIREY IIIF Mk IIIB S1479, 440 Flight, HMS *Hermes*, September 1931

RC09

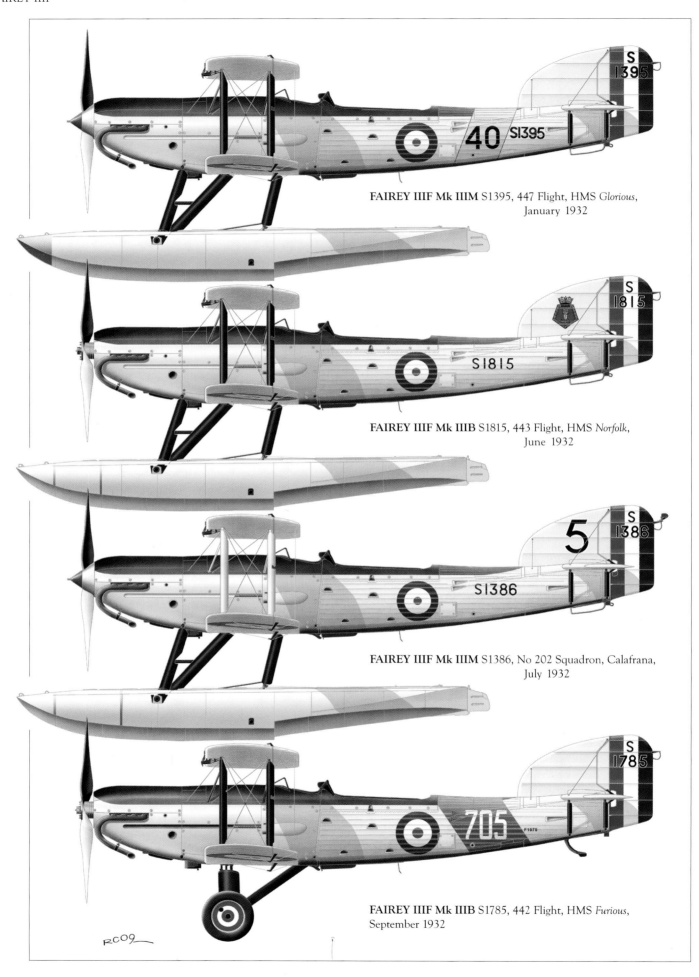

FAIREY IIIF Mk IIIM S1395, 447 Flight, HMS *Glorious*,
January 1932

FAIREY IIIF Mk IIIB S1815, 443 Flight, HMS *Norfolk*,
June 1932

FAIREY IIIF Mk IIIM S1386, No 202 Squadron, Calafrana,
July 1932

FAIREY IIIF Mk IIIB S1785, 442 Flight, HMS *Furious*,
September 1932

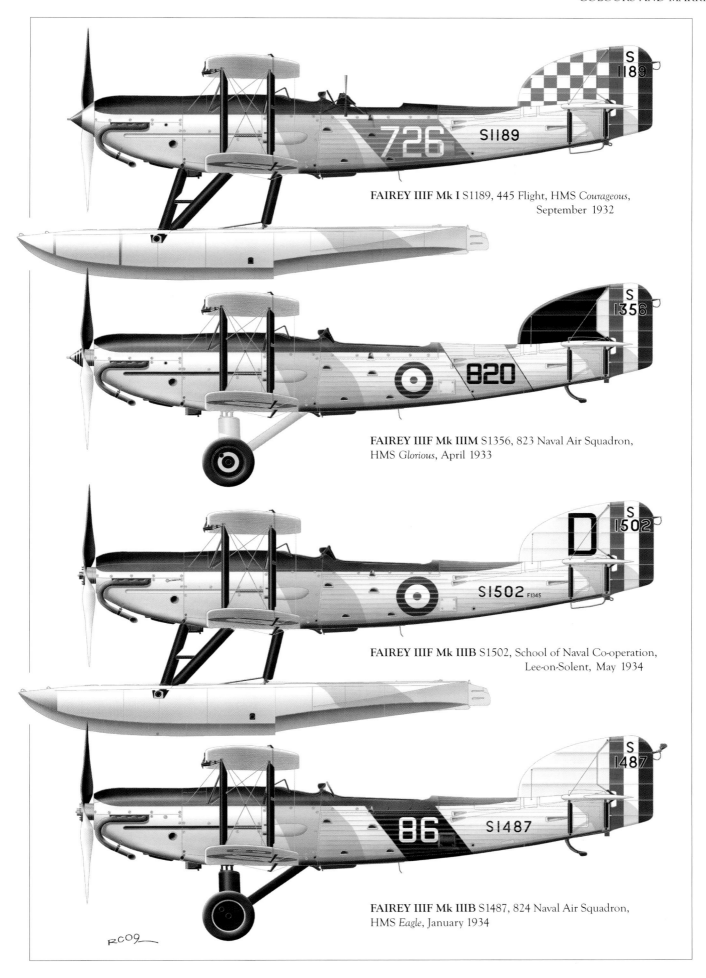

FAIREY IIIF Mk I S1189, 445 Flight, HMS *Courageous*,
September 1932

FAIREY IIIF Mk IIIM S1356, 823 Naval Air Squadron,
HMS *Glorious*, April 1933

FAIREY IIIF Mk IIIB S1502, School of Naval Co-operation,
Lee-on-Solent, May 1934

FAIREY IIIF Mk IIIB S1487, 824 Naval Air Squadron,
HMS *Eagle*, January 1934

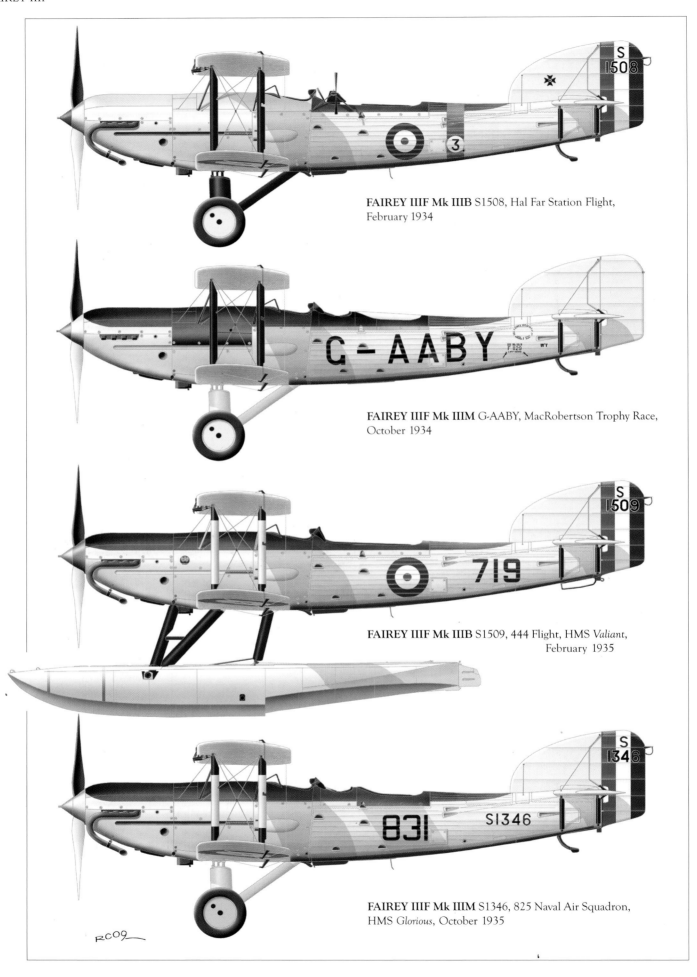

FAIREY IIIF Mk IIIB S1508, Hal Far Station Flight, February 1934

FAIREY IIIF Mk IIIM G-AABY, MacRobertson Trophy Race, October 1934

FAIREY IIIF Mk IIIB S1509, 444 Flight, HMS *Valiant*, February 1935

FAIREY IIIF Mk IIIM S1346, 825 Naval Air Squadron, HMS *Glorious*, October 1935

RC09